for Sonia Gernes

You hear the wings of the
        butterfly, dead,
A wash of light its shroud.
You guess what the wild rose sings,
The waterfall's splintered cloud;.
Read the dawn text of fuschia rings
Around islands. Your heart, once vowed,
Stirs to greet the gold of mid-August
                        wheat.
Gentle as dandelion fuzz, discreet,
Companion of cricket, friend of leaf,
Franciscan always through joy
                or grief;
Sonia, your sandal prints
                proclaim
The rightness of your name.

        The Lord bless and
        keep you forever
            Bernetta Quinn,
                O. S. F.
        August 31, 1988

AMERICAN POETS PROFILE SERIES

Courtesy of *The Houston Chronicle*

Heart's Invention

On the Poetry of Vassar Miller

Edited by Steven Ford Brown

Ford-Brown & Co., Publishers
Houston, Texas   1988

American Poets Profile Number 5
First Printing, January 1988.

Library of Congress Cataloguing in Publication Data

Brown, Steven Ford, 1952--
    Heart's Invention: On the Poetry of
    Vassar Miller

The American Poets Profile Series

Library of Congress Catalog Card Number: 86-82117
ISBN: 0-918644-49-6 Cloth
ISBN: 0-918644-48-8 Paper

9 8 7 6 5 4 3 2

Printed in the United States of America

The publication of this book is supported by a grant
from the Texas Commission on the Arts and the National Endowment for the Arts in Washington, DC, a
Federal Agency.

Acknowledgments

Grateful acknowledgement is made to the following magazines and presses for permission to reprint material originally appearing in their publications:

"Vassar Miller: Modern Mystic" is reprinted with permission from *Latitude 30° 18'*. Copyright © 1982 by *Latitude 30° 18'*.

"An Interview with Vassar Miller" is reprinted from *The Pawn Review*, Volume VII, Number 1. Copyright © 1983 by *The Pawn Review*.

The quote by Paul Christensen on the back cover is reprinted from *The Texas Observer*. Copyright © 1983 by *The Texas Observer*.

The quote by James Wright on the back cover is from *Poetry*, copyrighted © 1961 by the Modern Poetry Association, and is reprinted with permission by the Editor of *Poetry*.

Editor's Note

In editing a book such as this, there is usually a great deal of research; there are also literary people to talk to, editors and publishers to correspond with, and various literary matters that have to be arbitered and resolved. All of these things have been true in the course of this book. The fact that this project received one of the highest possible ratings from the Literature Panel of the Texas Commission on the Arts is testimony to the intense interest that people in Texas have in the poetry of Vassar Miller. This intense interest made my task easier; however, in some ways, it just made my task more difficult.

A number of contributors to this book have noted that Vassar Miller has yet to received the critical attention that her work deserves. This problem has now been corrected with the publication of this book. The American Poets Profile Series presents younger American poets with the unique opportunity to select an older American poet and discuss their work through the medium of a book-length consideration.

There were numerous and unusual problems that created difficulties in the course of editing this book. Each obstacle was a bridge to cross, and there were a number of people who either helped to construct that bridge or at least lent me a map. To those individuals I must offer some thanks: Jean Paul Batiste of the Texas Commission on the Arts for a steady hand and his personal interest in this project; Elizabeth Wachendorfer of the University of Houston, whose personal interest in this project began when I wandered into her office in search of a videotape; Robert Bonazzi for friendship, well-timed advice, and long conversations into the night about the nature and evolution of Texas literature; Pat Bozeman and the University of Houston's Special Collections for access to the Vassar Miller papers; to Larry McMurtry for bringing Vassar Miller to the attention of everyone in Texas with his speech in 1981 at the Fort Worth Art Museum, which was later reprinted in *The Texas Observer* as "Ever a Bridegroom: Reflections on the Failure of Texas Literature;" and, lastly, to Vassar Miller for her magnificent gifts.

Contents

Preface

LARRY MCMURTRY

I almost never talk about poetry. I'm a novelist and screen writer, and I talk a lot about the novel and the screen play. I think it's recognized by almost everyone that has much experience in writing that poets are the thoroughbreds and Arabians of language, and novelists are the plow horses. Throughout literary history there has been a constant stream of envy starting with novelists and running toward poets. Most novelists are jealous of poets to put it more simply. Faulkner said this very clearly. He said he was a "failed poet," and his miserable books of poems bear that out. Hemingway published some fairly horrible poetry.

You probably have to be a scholar to know this, but throughout the nineteenth century, novelists were just as jealous of poets as they are now. Dickens wrote poetry, Thackery wrote poetry, George Eliot wrote poetry. You can take it back in English literature at least to Fielding of the examples of novelists who have written bad poetry. I haven't committed much bad poetry, fortunately, but I have always been conscious because I do visit the universities and am constantly doing writing workshops. It always staggers me when I see children (children being freshmen and sophomores in college) attempting to write poetry and short stories. I think the theory behind teaching poetry and short stories at such an early age is that it's probably easier for a young person to write something short than it is to write something long. Unfortunately, exactly the opposite is true. It's much easier to work in a loose form like the novel. The novel is a compendious form which can survive a great many mistakes in language. Writers like Theodore Dreiser wrote terrible prose, but his books survive because of the breadth and depth of his sense of life. There are plenty of other examples in literary history of novelists who were not great prose stylists, yet somehow their books survived because of the vitality of their intellect and vision. It's perfectly possible for a novel to have vast mistakes in it. *War and Peace* has chapters that are very slow going and yet survive because of their overall vitality. But it's not possible for a lyric poem to survive unless the language is refined to the highest possible degree.

One thing that I've been puzzling over more and more now that I'm a middleaged novelist is the question of survival--the question of survival not just as a person, but as an artist. I think this is a question that doesn't get talked about or perhaps doesn't get thought about very often, because when you think about it, the conclusions you may draw are rather bleak.

I really enjoyed writing fiction for about fifteen years. I liked getting up every morning, I liked going to the typewriter, and I liked the words and characters that came out, that rolled out on the page. I might very rapidly turn against the books once I published them. I almost always become aware of their shortcomings. Nontheless, I really liked the activity of writing as I did it day-to-day for about fifteen years. And then I ceased to like it day-to-day as I did it. At that point in my career I began to give serious thought to the question of survival as an artist.

Here in America the whole training and thrust of Americanism inclines you to feel that you go out, you get educated, you learn a craft, and then you work at it and get better and better at it the rest of your life. Unfortunately, art does not work that way. It's not a progressive thing. It's much more natural that after a certain period of intensity or vitality that you begin to get worse at it. This is certainly true of novelists. Once I got obsessed with this question of survival, I made a study of the life spans and working careers of the major novelists, and it was an extremely sobering experience. It seems to me that about the most novelists get is ten or twelve years. Now they may go on working much longer than that. Many do go on working much longer than that--sometimes to their sorrow--but their most intense and best work is usually done within a rather short time span. Think back through literary history and conjure up the names of all the people who haven't survived to be middleaged. And if you apply that test to poets, all the poets who didn't make it as long as Vassar Miller has made it, the roll would be lengthy. But I can give you a few off the top of my head: Sidney, Marlowe, Byron, Shelley, Keats, Lorca, Pushkin, and Hart Crane. Survival is a complicated business, and I would think (and I speak with a good deal of humility here) it becomes a more difficult matter when you're working with a more difficult form.

The poem, the lyric poem, is easily the most concentrated form of literary activity. It requires the most intense sensitivity, not just to language (certainly to language) but I think also to human experience. It is essentially an effort to boil down one person's response to the vast complexity of human experience into a very few words and cadences. That kind of concentration, I think, must be excruciating. I'm very often glad that I'm not a lyric poet. I do not have to summon up that kind of concentration day-to-day.

For reasons that are totally mysterious to me, in some generations poets seem to survive fairly well for a long time. I think it's really rare for anybody to write well into old age. There are a few examples of people who have kept on, kept up their disciplines, and who have sort of chugged along, and who are rewarded for this with a late great period. I think Yeats was one; I think William Carlos Williams was another, but it's a rarity. It doesn't happen very often in any of the literary arts. It's almost unheard of for novelists to write well after they're sixty years old. They may write with fluency, but fluency is not the same thing as depth. And it may be that this kind of concentration that the lyric poem requires is no longer possible.

I've developed this theory which may or may not be true. You're striving for two things when you work over a long period in the arts. You're striving to survive for one thing, that is with your faculties intact, as J.D. Salinger would say; you're trying to survive. But you're also trying to get better. You don't want to just turn out more work. You want to write something that's better than what you've already written. It's a dreadful curse for a writer to write his/her best book first. This happens to people. Sometimes they strike it so forcefully and with such potency in the first book. I think of authors like Walker Percy, Joseph Heller and Ralph Ellison as three contemporary examples that somehow, although they go on writing books that are good, there's a sense of having peaked. This sense of having peaked is a dreadful thing to come to as an artist who is highly concentrated and who has to read his/her own work every day as something to cope with. It's very unnatural to have to read one writer every day for twenty-five or thirty years. There are scholars who can make a life of reading someone like Shakespeare or Dante, but it's very hard to read one writer every single day for thirty years. Yet that's exactly what you do when you write. I'm sure that there must be days when Vassar gets tired of her own lines, when she gets bored with her own prosody, when she gets tired of her own themes, when she feels that she's worked all the variations on these themes that she can fruitfully work. The test of the artist, the long-lasting artist, it seems to me, comes when this point is reached--when the writing isn't the fresh, youthful, happy-go-lucky sort of low risk enterprise that it usually is for the first five or ten years. By the time you've committed twenty-five or thirty years of your life to a given art, there's really nothing else you can do. You're not equipped to stop and do something else. You're locked into it. Yet, if you're any good, if you've kept your sensitivity alive, what you really want to do is get better. And it seems to me that Vassar Miller has succeeded at that.

I met her twenty-six years ago when I came to Rice University to go to graduate school, and I was editing an anthology of younger writers. I didn't know whether she was a younger writer or an older writer at the time, but I went to meet her and we became friends. I think as I have watched her poetry for a long, long time, it's very easy to point out certain broad characteristics which I admire and which I imagine others also admire--her clarity, her precision, her intelligence, her honesty. But I want to mention one other quality that I think she has both as a person and as a poet. The two things merge, and that is her tenacity. It's not simply brute survival that a poet is involved with, although sometimes they are; it's more than that. It's a tenacity that has to be at one and the same time, physical, intellectual, and moral. I believe this tenacity is something that Vassar Miller is richly endowed with. She has survived. She has gotten better. The formality and virtuosity in the early poems and her interest in tight forms (what I think of as tight forms, immature that I am) like the sonnet, has broken down. She's more free now. She's more complicated. She's dealing with things that are at once simpler and more complex. To do that and get across the dreadful bridge of middle age with your vitality intact is quite an achievement. Look at the poets of the last generation who didn't make it across the bridge: Robert Lowell, John Berryman, Randall Jarrel, Anne Sexton, Sylvia Plath, Theodore Roethke--just to name the ones that I can think of off the top of my head. You've got to survive on two levels. Your soul has got to survive--your concern, your heart, your feelings. Your skills have got to survive too. Literary history is rich in examples in which poets managed to preserve one, but not the other.

Heart's Invention

Abbreviations

In citations of Miller's poetry, the following abbreviations are used.

AF	*Adam's Footprint*
WW	*Wage War on Silence*
MB	*My Bones Being Wiser*
OR	*Onions and Roses*
ICS	*If I Could Sleep Deeply Enough*
SC	*Small Change*
AN	*Approaching Nada*
SNP	*Selected and New Poems: 1950-1980*
SSC	*Struggling to Swim on Concrete*

Vassar Miller: Modern Mystic
FRANCES SAGE

Vassar Miller, a Texas poet, though not a poet of Texas, has written fine poetry for the last thirty years, but her poetry runs, for the most part, against the grain of contemporary American poetry, not regional nor rural, urban or suburban, beat or political. Much of it is religious, Christian. Unlike some imagists as Bly, Wright, or Snyder, Miller uses neither place, nature, the collective unconscious, or Eastern religions to reveal her religious longings or vision. She is very much a Christian poet, but her sources are more the sources of an Emily Dickinson, those personal, domestic scenes, scenes of her own isolation and experience.

I met Miller several years ago when researching a survey article on Texas women poets. (1) But I was struck, then, at how little her poetry had to do with Texas. Although she has lived all her life in Texas, nothing in her poetry evokes it. The sources of her poetry are her own religious needs and feelings. She could just as well live any place.

Miller and I visited for some time at that first meeting and have corresponded occasionally since then. When Joe Slate and I decided to found a literary journal, we both thought immediately of Vassar Miller as the first poet we would like to publish. I, also, wanted to write about her, to trace the development of her poetry, to understand that most extraordinary of paradoxes, a successfully modern religious poet. I call her a modern mystic. To examine her poetry is to trace a life, a life marked by her two great spiritual needs: to say the unsayable and to accept a life cut off from others. Both, in a sense, are the same need: to reach beyond the self, to communicate, with God, with others.

Vassar Miller was born in 1924 in Houston, Texas, where she has lived except for brief absences. She was born a victim of cerebral palsy, which has afflicted her all her life. Educated at home by her parents until junior high school, she eventually received B.S. and M.A. degrees from the University of Houston. She is a rather shy, friendly woman with intelligent eyes, warm, and interested in conversation. She somehow bridges the gap between a halting, forced speech and a quick, eager mind. One feels in talking with her, her need to communicate with others. In spite of her difficult speech she has taught at time and has even given poetry readings. Her poem "Introduction to a Poetry Reading," which prefaces her book *If I Could Sleep Deeply Enough,* seriously makes light of her handicap.

> I was born with my mod dress sewn
> / onto my body,
> stitched to my flesh,
> basted into my bones.
> I could never, somehow, take it all off
> to wash the radical dirt out.
> I even carry my own rock
> hard in my mouth,
> grinding it out bit by bit,
> So, bear me
> as I bear you,
> high, in the grace of greeting.

> (*ICS*, p. ix)

She has written only a few poems specifically on cerebral palsy victims: "The Spastic" ends with the lines

> to Golgothas of gaze
> whose dead bead never swerves
> from the one who sways

nailed upon his nerves. (2)

and "Spastics" from *If I Could Sleep Deeply Enough*
which details the twilight lives of many spastics who
neither live nor die young.

> Don't worry
> They just
> hang on
> drooling, stupid from watching too much TV,
> born-that-way-senile,
> rarely marry, expected to make it with Jesus,
> never really make it at all,
> don't know how,
> some can't
> feed themselves,
> fool with, *well*--Even some sappy saint said they
> look young because pure.
>
> (*ICS*, p. 39)

One is not surprised that much of her poetry concerns silence and dumbness, but Miller does not see her
affliction as the impetus to her poetry. "I'd write poetry
regardless." Whether that is true cannot, of course, be
tested. What is clear is that her handicap combined with
her religious background have set the constraints and
directions of her life. The theme of acceptance often
appears in the early work as a need for her to accept
herself, the constraints of her life. But acceptance is not
limited just to self-acceptance. Often, especially in some
of the mid and later poems, she implores God to accept
her.

She thinks that her religious feelings have been the
greatest single influence and source of her poetry. She
has always been religious, starting as a child when a
maid took her to evangelistic meetings in a tent. At
various times she has attended the Presbyterian church

(the church of her parents) and the Episcopalian church (whose liturgy she still loves). But for some years she has belonged only to the Covenant Baptist Church in Houston, which, though a part of the Southern Baptist Conference, is not, Miller thinks, rigorous in its tenets. The membership is varied and seems made up of people who have come there from other churches. Miller feels most accepted there.

Yet, even though she has always been a part of an organized church, Miller's religious feelings, as expressed in her poetry, reflect no particular theology. Based, of course, in Christianity, the poetry belongs to the mystical tradition of religious verse. Usually intense, her religious poetry traces her prayers, her doubts, and finally her role as the mystic poet. Always the theme of the naked self, trying to say the unsayable unfolds in the poems. If the dominant theme of the poetry is the impossibility of saying, the inevitable dumbness of the self before God and fellow creatures, then her poetry itself does say, does try at least to say, in words, the unsayable, does deny, if not the difficulty, at least the impossibility of breaking self-isolation.

An early poem, "Without Ceremony," which prefaces her book *Wage War on Silence* sets many of the themes found in later poems. (3)

> Except ourselves, we have no other prayer;
> Our needs are sores upon our nakedness.
> We do not have to name them; we are here.
> And You who made the eye can see no less.
> We fall, not on our knees, but on our hearts,
> A posture humbler far and more downcast;
> While Father Pain instructs us in the arts
> Of praying, hunger is the worthiest fast.
> We find ourselves where tongues cannot
>   / wage war
> On silence (farther, mystics never flew)

But on the common wings of what we are,
Borne on the wings of what we bear,
    / toward You,
Oh Word, in whom our wordiness dissolves,
When we have not a prayer except ourselves.

                           (*WW*, p. 3)

Like much of her work, the poem has a passionate intensity, feeling forced through form, revealing in the triumph of successful form the need to triumph by the will into words. Interwoven in the poem are Miller's essential concerns: silence or dumbness, suffering, nakedness of the essential self, her relationship to God, and acceptance.

Many of her poems reveal the paradox of saying the unsayable, breaking the silence while asserting it, establishing the communion in the solitary act of writing. Silence and the ineffable feelings are almost always based in her relation to God. From the rather ordered poems of her early work to her freer, more recent work, silence and God intertwine. Naturally her religious poetry has many facets, but it is her coming to a mystical vision that develops in her poetry.

Her early religious poems, like the later, often disclose the dark side, the human condition as it is. She somehow manages to affirm, by acceptance, that condition. In her early sonnet "Fantasy on the Resurrection"

Flaws cling to flesh as dews cling to a rose:
The cripples limp as though they would prolong,
Walking, a waltz; the deaf ears, opened, close
As if their convolutions hear all song;
The blind eyes keep half shut as if to fold
A vision fast men never glimpse by staring.
Against their will the mute lips move that hold
A language which was never tongue's for sharing.
Shocked shag of earth and everything thereunder

> Turned inside out--the nail--gnarled have
> / caught Heaven
> Like a bright ball. Not in their reknit wonder,
> But in their wounds lies Christ's sprung
> / grace engraven-
> Not in the body lighter than word spoken,
> But in the side still breached, the hands
> / still broken.
>
> (*WW*, p. 17)

It is as though the grace given requires the suffering, reversing the usual pattern of redemption. Just as the dew clings to the rose before it evaporates so the physical flaws cling to the flesh. Through the flaws the grace can be imagined. In some sense the flawed body has the mark of grace and thus the flaws become an enhancement like the dew on the rose. While the poem makes the claim confidently, the title casts the doubt. And the ambiguity flows through the poem. Is it a fantasy that the flawed are truly graced and should affirm their brokenesss? Or can it be true? The doubt and hope combine. In the early poetry some sort of faith tries to sustain acceptance.

In his review of *Wage War on Silence* (*New York Times Book Review*, February 26, 1961) Dudley Fitts says of "Though He Slay Me" that the twenty lines "sing a totality of torment and acceptance with a power that one will not soon forget . . ." In that poem Miller pleads with God to "Still tell me no, my God, and tell me no/Till I repeat the syllable for a song. . . ." She wants the "no" to hold for her the same implicit promise that Good Friday brings of Easter. Again the reversal. The continuous no will not be a denial of her but rather the means toward her acceptance, her ultimate resurrection. Her faith will have to be worked at-- no easy union with God can be possible. And the poem's end completes the reversal:

No, no, still, the echo of Your yes
Distorted among the crevices and caves
Of the coiled ear which deep in its abyss
Resolves to music all Your negatives.

(*WW*, p. 60)

Though the themes of silence and dumbness are not
overhelming in these two early religious poems, the idea
persists in both. In "Fantasy on the Resurrection" the
lines "Against the will the mute lips move that hold/a
language which was never tongues for sharing. . . ."
alludes both to the dumb's need to speak and the
language that is the essential self, an unsayable language. In "'Though He Slay Me'" the silence is the
hush, the dark promise "Between Good Friday's dusk
and Easter day. . . ." It is the necessary silence to be
filled by the promising no.

In her next book, *My Bones Being Wiser*, three of
her religious poems again affirm the bleak silence of
God. In "A Dream from the Dark Night" the poem's
speaker is St. John of the Cross. He describes giving up
his last earthly attachment, St. Teresa's letters.

and so take them and burn them
While I turn to You, O my God, my bruised feet
leaping the meadows of Your flesh
to the desert of darkness
where Your silence speaks so loud
I cannot hear You.

(*MB*, p. 51)

The turning of God alone through great effort is urged
for herself in "Resolve."

I must go back to the small place,
to the swept place,

to the still place,
to the silence

there bathe my hands and my heart
in the hush. . . .

(*MB*, p. 65)

And in "Loneliness" she tries not only to accept it but
to affirm it.

This silence, this crying,
O my God, is my country
with Yours the sole footstep besides my own.
Save me amid its landscapes
so terrible, strange
I am almost in love with them!

(*MB*, p. 67)

While the verse is freer in *My Bones Being Wiser*,
the intensity of feeling is still pushed into form even as
it was in the early sonnets. In *The New York Times
Book Review* (June 21, 1964) Denise Levertov thought
that a few of the poems were weakened by sentimentality but that many are "notably spare, taut, and exact.
They have a timeless sound" which "arises very directly
out of a life, without being filtered through a highly
charged intellectual environment."

By the time of her collection *Onions and Roses*,
Miller has reached a calmness, sometimes hopeful, sometimes seemingly despairing. Again the themes of mute-
ness, silence, and the search for an acceptance often
unfold themselves in direct address to God. The calmness finds expression in "Cologne Cathedral" in which
the beauty of the Cathedral in the night seems to
"speak" Miller's need to have communion with God.

I came upon it stretched against the starlight,
a black lace

of stone. What need to enter and kneel down?
It said my prayers for me,

lifted in a sculptured moment of imploring
God in granite,
rock knees rooted in depths where all men
ferment their dreams in secret.

Teach marble prayers to us who know no longer
what to pray,
like this dumb worship's lovely gesture carven
from midnight's sweated dews.

(OR, p. 21)

But even the calm, mildly hopeful tone has a bleak side
as revealed in the lines, "Teach. . .to us who know no
longer/what to pray. . . ." And the calmness turns out
to be a surface illusion, a calmness of form masking
despair as in "DeProfundis."

O Lord, defend me when I go
Through the dark in daylight.
Be with me when I smile peaceably
though tigers tear at my guts.

Stay with me who talk to my friends
as an earless monster
winks at me; comfort me, starved and
        / black-tongued,
though I eat at dainty tables.

Stand by when snowfalls of words melt in
deserts of my deafness.
Sustain me, though morning after morning,
I take life from You like death.

Accept me, though I give myself

> like a cast-off garment
> to a tramp, or like an idiot's
> bouquet of onions and roses.
>
> > (*OR*, p. 29)

This time she implores Him to accept her. In the earlier poems she often struggled as much with self-acceptance as with a reaching out for God's acceptance. Her prayers then were for strength to embrace the self even as she sought God. Now some measure of acceptance must surely have come, for the struggle for self-acceptance is notable in its absence. Even though the poems are often bleak, some plateau has been reached. One expects later poems to move even further in the direction of reconciliation.

But the expectation is not fulfilled. Even allowing for thematic selection her next book, *If I Could Sleep Deeply Enough*, frightens with its grim vision. The hard won, seeming acceptance found in earlier books breaks. There is the bleakness of "Another Day."

> The day, damp bird, mopes on its branch
> > / where leaves
> still cling with wizened fists above
> the lawns all blanched the color of stale vomit.
>
> The day drops dead, time's tune inside my skull
> droning toward sleep when I lie down
> lonely to lust's one-finger exercise.
>
> > (*ICS*, p. 4)

And God has vanished. Or if not vanished, no longer invoked, no longer the intimate companion of her poetic-religious thoughts. He is present more by indirection. Death seems closer to her, more often in her thoughts. And even acceptance of death comes as a dwindling down of poetic possibilities in "Minor Miner."

One time
the poems lay loose like gold nuggets
spilling out of the pores of my skin.

Now I
hurtle down shafts of myself,
having become an abandoned mine,

where in
the dark, I, my lamp gone out,
wait for the welding of rock with my bone.

(*ICS*, p. 47)

The grimness of the vision in *If I Could Sleep
Deeply Enough* breaks through the form. Despair has a
passionate voice. One can see the change by comparing
the shaping voice in "Fait Accompli," a poem from
Onions and Roses, with "Now You See Me, Now. . . ."

FAIT ACCOMPLI

I sit while loneliness
Seeps slowly through my skin.
Waiting, I try to guess
Which one of us will win--

I or the gaunt black wolf
Who crouches in some lair
Of corner, cranny, shelf,
Ready to pounce and tear.

What need to ask when vein
Has felt the burning claws
Slash open so that pain
Beats where the heart once was?

(*OR*, p. 68)

NOW YOU SEE ME, NOW. . . .

How I race
on the back of a beast
rearing high on a heatwave's footless hold!

I must fall,
I must sink, must go down,
smothered inside his red belly of rage.

(*ICS*, p. 42)

Even though the two poems share some of the same feeling, the latter poem in its spareness has a burst of feeling unmatched in the earlier one.

Death as a dwindling down becomes a way to show the isolation, the silence in *Small Change*. It even becomes part of a domestic scene in "Homecoming Blues."

The ashes have waited for me in the ash tray,
but say nothing.
The towel hanging on the rack that I have
/ longed to see
somehow says nothing.
My dogs who have already forgotten how
/ much they missed me
say nothing either.
    And O O O O
    I wish I could call my mother
or eat death like candy.

(*SC*, p. 17)

While not all poems in *Small Change* are grim, or speak of death or silence, some extend the themes. One wonders where Miller could turn after a poem like "Momento Mori," which is in memory of Anne Sexton.

You think that I am smiling,
but I'm practicing my death-grin.
I must wear it for a rather long time.

You think that I am sleeping,
but I'm developing my grave skills
for when I must do death's motionless ballet.

You think that I am breathing,
but I'm toning up my death-gasp.
I owe it to my friends to do one thing right.

You think that I am resting,
but I'm hunched over my decay,
which makes do for the pretty baby I wasn't.

(SC, p. 12)

If we had no more poems to explore we might fear that Miller could see no way out of the death vision. Yet a chapbook of poetry, not a collection but one long poem, offers the hope of a new direction. Again it is the religious feeling, vision, which comes forward to sustain her. It is in *Approaching Nada* that Miller finds her poetic role of mystic poet. The long poem defines the new relation to God and silence.

IV

Abbe Bremond, you wrote,
"Le poete, c'est un mystique manque."
An aborted mystic,
a frustrated mystic,
or did you mean,
simply, a sorry one?
Doubtless the latter, since
the poet like the mouse will scuttle
clean to the border

of the ineffable,
then scurry back
with tidbits of the Vision.
Whereas Juan de la Cruce,
say, or Teresa de Avila
leap once and for all
headlong into darkness,
drowning in dumbness,
dying Shakespearean lovers.
Mon seigneur, I wonder--
Christ's Gospel spelled these self-same saints,
"Go tell. What's whispered in your closets
shout from your rooftops.
Follow me who flaunt my body's banner
crimson before the bulls."
These poets of the Nada
obeyed Him. So, poets, mystics of
/ the bruising thing
climb up blood concretes
to leave nailed high
white pieces of themselves.

(*SNP*, p. 124)

Even though the poem reaches a climax in this fourth section, the poem has a fifth and final section that offers a way out of the grim vision, a new perspective. Through memory and in history she can place herself. She links her personal past to her family past in the South and finds a place in the continuum of history. Section V begins,

Although I wander
down hallways of my body, ghost
prowling passages of my blood
to my most hidden corners, still
I know my name.
I trace footprints. . . .

and ends with

> . . .a tree rooted
> but in God's chancy hand. Middling-good ghost,
> I seek my roots of shifted waters
> shifting toward nada.
>
> (*SNP*, p. 126)

For a time, at least, acceptance of the self, of silence, and of death have been found in her role as mystical poet and searcher of the past.

The poems since *Approaching Nada* are more various. But some of the new hope, the new acceptance is in them. The recent poems in *Selected and New Poems 1950-1980* work themselves out in personal memories or in considerations of placing death in some greater context. The tone has changed for the most part and the style is more naked, more direct. If sometimes Miller speaks directly to the reader of her condition, she speaks only frankly, not with rancor, as in "Summation" and "Dramatic Monologue in the Speaker's Own Voice." The tone in all the recent poems is calmer, more assured. She explores over and over the theme of death but now without despair.

The calm tone is reflected even in her flashes of humor. The grim humor of "Homecoming Blues" of putting her lonely misery into a ragtime "O O O O" changes into the whimsical imaging of the mind as a turtle or the punning of "The Master of the Cosmos."

In these later poems on death, she ranges from the playfullness of "Wild Child" and "Senility" to the rather grim understanding of "Another Sleep Poem."

> Sleep seduces me
> better than the lovers that I never had
> ever could.

Sleep can comfort me
better than shabby prayers I always say
never do.

Sleep can console me
better than alcohol that rakes my guts
ever will.

But, friends, best of all,
far more than death sleep soothes me,
when, during the night, we wake to kiss
            / each other--
Death has no mouth.

                                        (*SNP*, p. 156)

While in *Approaching Nada* Miller linked death to
history and memory, she now links hope to them also.
In her recent poems she has moved beyond acceptance,
beyond embracing death to the other side. Her vision
affirms the Christian faith in redemption. The title poem
of the section in *Selected and New Poems 1950-1980*
entitled *The Sun Has No History, New Poems, 1977-1980*
ends not just on a note of acceptance but on a note of
hope. If sun, water, air have no sin, lacking history and
memory, they also have no hope in themselves. It is
only the mortal human with his burden of original sin,
with his past, who can imagine a future, while living in
the moment, who can leap up to hope.

THE SUN HAS NO HISTORY

The sun has no history,
the leaves keep no diary,
that bird on that limb feels no nostalgia,
nor did the water remember the slosh of
            / our feet,
my sister's and mine, in the worn wash tub,

nor did the hot wax of air take the imprint
of my aunt's chuckling voice,
"Land sakes! You all sing it like a dirge,"
Revive Us Again, which she had heard lively.
No, because days are sculptured from space,
shaped out of sizzling motes,
hammered from heat-waves.

Seasons repeat themselves,
babble syllables innocent of order.
Hours leave no fingerprints
for sleuths of memory to trace.
Last year camouflages itself
under the light of this instant
slanting upon me who comb
the green of this bush,
the red of that bloom,
the stuff of clouds overhead here
turning to me forever
familiar faces of strangers.

The sun has no history.
Only I, bearing
my Adam and Eve on my back,
dragging under, dragged down, may leap
up to the saddle of hope.

(*SNP*, p. 149)

An Interview with Vassar Miller
KARLA HAMMOND

KH: Vassar, what attitude of your parents has most influenced your writing?
VM: My father, being of a literary bent, most influenced my writing. When I was about eight, he would lug home his big office typewriter for me to play with. I have always been intrigued by machines and devices that helped me work better than I did alone. So, I began to fool with it and found myself interested in rhymes and turns of phrases. My father would read and criticize my efforts. I remember winning a radio contest for a poem about a local brand of ice cream. My first draft praised the product, "as mellow as old cream." "God, no!" Daddy protested. "That would mean the ice cream was sour." On another occasion in a poem about the moon, I wrote, "I would be acquaint with thee." My father said that I was trite and so I flushed the poem down the toilet.

My earliest poem though, was to my young step-mother. In it I referred to "your hair of gray." "But my hair isn't gray. It's black," she protested, being all of nineteen or twenty. "I couldn't think of a rhyme for black," I told her.

KH: To change the subject a bit--to speak of another influence. . ."She apparently is a Roman Catholic and her book contains extremely dense and rich religious verse" (Webster Schoot about Vassar Miller). Why do you feel he felt so certain about Catholicism? For me, your work doesn't reflect the inflexibility or dogmatic nature of Catholicism. Your father's father was a Catholic--"My father also/told me how his father,/stern German, devout Catholic. . ."

VM: I guess Schoot assumed that I was a Catholic because I use Catholic imagery in my poetry--the Eucharist, the Host, the altar, etc. Much of my religious imagery is simply Biblical. Yes, my paternal grandfather was Catholic.

KH: Yet, I know from an earlier interview (in *Poetry Now*) and other biographical statements, that you are now affiliated with the Covenant Baptist Church. How has this church helped change your poems? What are the greatest differences between Episcopalian faith and Baptist as manifest in your own religious experience?

VM: Episcopalian and Baptist churches are expressions of the same Christian faith. Historically, the Episcopal Church is hieratical and the Baptist churches (it is incorrect to speak of the Baptist Church) is free; i.e., each congregation is autonomous. Often Baptist churches in the South are fundamentalistic. Covenant, however, is liberal. Also, it has adopted some "Catholic" features. For example, we follow the church year. Really, however, I joined Covenant because I liked the make-up of the congregation, the openmindedness, the emphasis on good music and the arts. I still love the Episcopal Church, however, with its liturgy and its emphasis on the sacraments. I don't know that the change in churches has affected my religious experience so much as the other way around. The change was more for personal than theological reasons.

KH: In speaking of style (in writing), which is also a personal factor, what qualities of language or circumstance make possible the fusing of the sensual and spiritual love that Dudley Fitts attributed to your work?

VM: Sensual and spiritual love are often used as metaphors for each other in much religious poetry, particularly Catholic mystical poetry and religious experience. The Song of Solomon in the Old Textament is a frank celebration of sexual love, but it has been viewed as an allegory of love between Christ and the Church or between Christ and the individual soul. Other poets who have used this symbolism are Donne, Crashaw, and Herbert.

KH: How do you see Donne, Crashaw, and Herbert using this symbolism differently, or is it difficult to discern because of the Metaphysical influence--that fusing of sensual imagery and religious passion?

VM: I don' think these poets use this symbolism any differently. When Donne says, "Or ever chaste except You ravish me," he's using the same sexual imagery as, say St. John of the Cross. Of course, whoever wrote the Song of Solomon was writing a straight love poem. It was the Church Fathers who gave it the allegorical interpretation.

KH: Earlier you spoke of liturgy. Would you say that your use of a formal language and syntax is derived from liturgy?

VM: No, maybe it's the other way around. Liturgy has always seemed to me the poetry of worship, humanity's poor best for the infinite. Formal language and syntax have always been my personal struggle for order in what has often seemed my disorderly world.

KH: Three-line stanzas seem to be a favorite form for you. Is there a particular reason for this?

VM: The three-line stanza is simply another, though simpler, attempt at order. Often, you will note, I count syllables.

KH: Yes, I was aware of that discipline. In speaking of poetry you've said "it seems the fashion, anymore, to be formless or devoid of any traditional forms." Do you see *vers libre* as devoid of form? What are your favorite traditional forms? The sonnet? One reviewer in *Quarry* (Winter 1965) noted that there were twenty-one sonnets in *My Bones Being Wiser* and *Wage War on Silence*.

VM: No, good free verse is not formless any more than a spider web is. A good free verse poem weaves its form out of itself. But much of what passes for poetry today reads like a grocery list or a postcard, as if the poet slapped down the first words that came to mind without benefit of passion or precision. I never really thought of my favorite traditional form. I guess it is the sonnet, or maybe just the simple well-wrought lyric.

KH: Would you say the "lyric" form was basic to the early poetry you were introduced to as a child?

VM: Yes, especially hymns. In fact, an early ambition was to become a hymn-writer. The notebooks of my adolescence are filled with miserable imitations of equally miserable hymns.

KH: Getting back to orderlessness. . .What are some of the factors you feel that have contributed to the fashionable chaos of contemporary poetry?

VM: It seems to me that in the sixties, with the God-is-Dead movement in theology, the human became exalted to the point of the absurd so that every human product became holy and hence beautiful. Tin cans and toilet seats became *objets d'arts*. Words, also, didn't have to be arranged with craft, just whatever came naturally. There's a good side to this trend, of course; too much artifice stifles, the letter killeth, and all that. But enough is enough.

KH: What for you are the basic distinctions between prose and poetry?

VM: There are fewer close repetitive patterns in prose. In poetry, by and large, the language is more for its own sake. Of course, in poetry you have the ballad and the narrative poem and the verse play. But even in these forms it seems to me that you dwell more on the language than in the short story or the novel. What about *Ulysses*? I confess I don't know what to say. I tried to read it and gave up.

KH: What constitutes craft for you?

VM: Craft for me is putting together words, phrases, and sentences in the best way. It is the loving use of language. More specifically, it means getting the right rhythm for the particular poem, the most precise words for what I mean, making sure my metaphors are apt, not strained or mixed, making sure I don't have too many adjectives, trying always for fresh language, trying to make the poem a unified whole.

KH: In reading over a number of reviews of your work, I've frequently encountered the term "virtuoso" by those who attribute it to your work and those who deny its relevance. How would you define this term in its practical application to poetry writing? And what *place* do you feel it holds in writing? Is it a legitimate issue?

VM: If "virtuoso" means one who has great technical skill in what he/she does, I hope the term fits me. To me it means the ability to write well, then. Hand me that dictionary, over there, will you, so I can look up "virtuoso." It's one of those words I assume I know until I'm asked to define it. Well, by definition it means one skilled in. . .an art: connoisseur, aesthete, dilettante, expert, adept, artist, etc. I've always thought of the term as applied to a violinist who can do all sorts of fancy work with his bow. In this sense, I've never thought of myself as a virtuoso, though I often feel like a juggler, since I must keep so many factors in mind.

KH: What other qualities are crucial to one's writing besides symmetry, objectivity, intellect, irony, integrity and wit?

VM: Deep feeling is crucial, and some sort of embracing vision of life. Not that one can be always consistent, or maybe even should, since a poet is writing poetry, reflecting life as he/she sees it at a given moment, not philosophy or theology. But I don't see how a good poet or writer of any kind can be a creature of whim or sensation.

KH: Do you recognize intellect and passion in poetry as identical? What makes this possible?

VM: A poem results from a fusion of intellect and passion, is the fruit of their union. What makes this possible is the nature of the poem itself. A poem is not made out of ideas alone or of feeling alone. Otherwise we have essay or emoting, not poetry.

KH: A number of critics have spoken of paradox being at the heart of your poetry. Would you say that paradox lies at the root of all poetry that presents the ambiguities of unities and conflicting polarities in a vision that is flexible and open-ended? In his article "The Language of Paradox" appearing in Criticism: The Foundations of Modern Literary Judgement (1), Cleanth Brooks stated: "There is a sense in which paradox is the language appropriate and inevitable to poetry. It is the scientist whose truth requires a language purged of every trace of paradox; apparently the truth which the poet utters can be approached only in terms of paradox."

VM: I agree that paradox is at the root of all poetry, because poetry is about life as we perceive it and that sort of life is ambiguous. Of course, some of modern science would seem to present paradoxes too--for example, light travels in waves and in particles. Maybe only God is really unambiguous. Or maybe God is the only one who doesn't worry about ambiguity!

KH: Speculating on the motives of God suggests something of the philosopher. What distinguishes the poet from the philosopher? (i.e., "Your ponderousness is nimbler than our nets;" from "On Receiving a Philosopher's Autograph")

VM: The poet writes from his/her own gut-perceptions of things more than the philosopher. The poet's perception is more transitory, but paradoxically more enduring because it's more universal. Love is love, for instance, whatever the culture, and that's what the poet writes about whether in modern America or ancient China. But philosophies of love may differ so as to seem to have no kinship whatever. However, "On Receiving a Philosopher's Autograph" is actually dedicated to Paul Tillich and I was referring to his style. That's another way, the most important way poet differs from philosopher. In a poem, style and content are one; in a philosophical treatise, such is not the case.

KH: "Because my gifts are selfish celebrations. . ." ("Not Going Away Gift: For Jenney and George"). Is poetry a selfish celebration? Why? How so?

VM: "Not Going Away Gift" merely expresses a wish that some friends of mine wouldn't leave Houston. In this sense the poem is a "selfish celebration." But I don't think the poetry is.

KH: You've spent most of your life in Houston, but has place had very little emphasis on what you write? Would you have dealt with the same themes no matter where you lived? Is place more important to a novelist than a poet?

VM: I would have dealt with the same themes wherever I lived. However, there are some natural events--cicadas, hurricanes, long hot summers, drab unexciting Januarys (no snow storms, few snows) that I wouldn't mention if I lived, say, in New England. Place is more important in the kind of novels I like. Still, I'm not sure. Place is awfully important to a poet like Frost.

KH: Is there anything that you would like to say about your working habits? Where you've done your best writing? Time of day? Season? Place?

VM: I do my best writing at home where I am relaxed and in familiar surrounds. "Approaching Nada" was written in Phoenix, and I consider it one of my best poems, but it is an exception. I often write in the morning, but not exclusively, and in my office where my typewriter is. I used to hold lines in my mind for a long time, even for years, before I used them. Now, though, I am not so lucky; I'm apt to forget them. So, I write them down. In recent years I've had long dry spells, broken by bouts of furious writing. Right now, however, I seem to be writing slowly, peacefully, as I did twenty years ago, maybe a poem a week. I hope this process can continue.

KH: Why do you think that "Approaching Nada" is one of your best poems? Do you see yourself speaking to a particular person in that poem?

VM: "Approaching Nada" is full of intensity. It came all at once. In writing it I wrote a poem a day until I realized that the individual poems were really sections of one poem. In "Approaching Nada" I feel I sort of summed myself up, defined where I am now. I guess I was writing for myself. Who else would care so much?

KH: Denise Levertov's saying that you write as someone who is not "looking to see if her peers are listening" seems to parallel your early habit of not sending out poems. Do you envision a particular audience reading your work? Wilbur speaks of one's poetry being addressed to a muse and that one purpose of the muse is to conceal the fact that poems aren't addressed to a specific person Would you agree?

VM: I don't think I write for a specific person. I think poets write to their deepest selves.

KM: Which contemporaries do you read frequently?

VM: I don't read many of my contemporaries very much now that I no longer review.

KH: Then, do you find yourself returning to earlier poets or, on the other hand, reading younger poets?

VM: I return to the older moderns or read whatever is at hand. Frankly, when I'm dry it depresses me to read poetry because I'm not writing it, and when I am writing it, I'm busy writing my own, although I do read more poetry at such times.

KH: How much of an influence (religious, meditative or otherwise) has Gerard Manley Hopkins had on your work?

VM: Hopkins used to have a great influence on my style. I would like the influence of his sprung rhythm, which I sense rather than understand, and the muscular strength of his lines.

KH: In saying "sense rather than understand" are you suggesting that intuition or instinct rests at the heart of poetry?

VM: No, I merely mean that I can feel rather than understand "sprung rhythm." I've read various definitions of it, but none completely get through to me.

KH: Do you feel that critics comparison of your work to Herbert's or Donne's is justified?

VM: I guess some of Donne's religious anguish is present in some of my early work. Maybe some of Herbert's fervor also. Not his serenity.

KH: What in your own life kept you from experiencing Herbert's sense of "serenity"?

VM: My inclination to doubt and question, my rebelliousness. Though now I recall some poems of Herbert's where he displays these qualities.

KH: To speak of a more recent influence or inspiration. . .How did Cynthia Macdonald's class (at the University of Houston) in poetry influence your writing?

VM: I wrote one poem, an imitation of sorts, of Macdonald's style. And she roused me briefly, to try new forms, new, that is, to me, but I don't think them too successful.

KH: Could you elaborate on these new forms? Was your poem ever published? What quality of imagination do you think imitation can engender in a poet practicing another's forms (style) and/or content?

VM: The only new form, really, if that, were the two poems in sections, "Letters to Friends Dead and Living" in *If I Could Sleep Deeply Enough*. The sectioning in "Approaching Nada" is another example. Macdonald read us examples of poems written in sections in her workshop and I decided to try it. The poem written in imitation of her style was published in a little magazine now defunct. To try to imitate a style is to understand it better.

KH: When asked how she would define imagination,

Denise Levertov said: "it is the power of perceiving analogies and of extending this power from the observed to the surmised. While fancy supposes, imagination believes, however, and draws kinetic force from the fervor of belief" (*The Southern Review*). How would you define imagination? I was very interested in this term in view of H.A. Maxson's saying of *Small Change*: "There are poems here that examine the particles of imagination that blunder through the air around us and are, occasionally, beautifully inhaled and rendered into poems."

VM: My definition of imagination would agree with Levertov's. I would add that imagination in writing is the power to put one's vision or experience into words and to enable a reader to share that vision or experience.

KH: Do you mean to differentiate between "vision" and "experience"?

VM: Not necessarily--though, I guess, one's experience determines one's vision.

KH: Has poetry or religion been the stay against darkness or madness as some poets are wont to say?

VM: I guess it would depend on the person as to whether religion, poetry, or another element had been the stay against madness or darkness. In my own case, I'd like to think religion has, and I think in some sense it has been. Maybe too it has been a brute determination to survive, or to the hope that tomorrow will be better, or at least different. Yet, I think that this attitude is based, however shakily, on faith.

KH: What do you discern to be the main poetic challenge of the time? The crisis of personality? Spirit or conscience? Or have we become a post-confessional literary society where the *objective correlative* may find meaning again?

VM: The poetic challenge of the time is what it has always been, to write with passion and precision. Poetry can do only what it can do. It is not religion. It is not ethics. It is not politics. It cannot substitute for any of these phenomena without distorting itself, not to mention whatever it tries to substitute for. But it can perform its own task well.

KH: "Although poets/grow beards, get drunk, and go to bed unmarried,/their imitators pull the selfsame antics/and never make it, because poems never/spring out of opium" ("Remembering Aunt Helen"). Could you elaborate on this contrast between poets and non-poets?

VM: Poets are supposed to "get drunk," etc. (I didn't mean ALL poets do, or have to), but a lot of would-be poets imitate the supposed excesses and eccentricities of real poets in a vain attempt to be the real thing. It was a mere humorous comment.

KH: Now to move from humor to doubt. . ."An Athenian Reminisces" suggest a certain skepticism (rather than cynicism). Would you say this is the price of getting older?

VM: The older I get the less sure I become. It's my price for getting older anyhow.

KH: You have four references to Bach: "Letter to Friends Dead and Living," "Enlightened Selfishness," "Exile," "German, 1976." Is Bach your favorite composer?

VM: Yes. Recently I wrote a poor poem to Bach that will never see print. I felt sad because I couldn't do better by him.

KH: Dudley Fitts speaks of the "lyric queerness that she (Miller) extracts from her soul-searching." How would you interpret the term "lyric queerness" and what is your response to his statement?

VM: I have no idea what Fitts means. My response is that he's entitled to his own opinion. Sometimes I think critics ought to write their own poems.

KH: Do you feel that a critic who is also a poet has a better understanding of the fundamentals of poetry?

VM: Yes.

KH: Reviewers have spoken of the heaviness or ungain-liness of the title--*Wage War on Silence.* Now nearly twenty years later do you have any particular feelings about this?

VM: I still like the title best of my titles, because I think that poetry does "wage war on silence"--both in the sense in which Edwin Arlington Robinson wrote, "Poetry is saying what cannot be said," and in the sense that in writing a poem I try to give expression to thoughts and feelings, never quite successfully. Valery said, "A poem is finally abandoned in despair."

KH: Do you have that sense of "despair" on finally leaving a poem? Is there never a sense of triumph as well in the paradox of "saying what cannot be said"?

VM: Of course, there's triumph. I think Valery was merely using a metaphor--saying that a good poet never fully realizes his intention and knows it.

KH: I'd like to discuss this idea of silence a little further. Could you elaborate on what you meant in saying "Somewhere between silence and ceremony springs/the Word" ("Approaching Nada")? Is this comparable to "a dialogue higher than sound" ("Oratory Sotto Voce")? Is this what you meant in praising "living in silence,/letting the leaves/breathe through me all men's/in no man's language" ("Precision")? Or "upon the branches of our silence hang our words,/half-ripen-ed, fruit" ("The Tree of Silence")? How does "Resolve" ("the silence under the absence of noise") relate to these poems? Do other poems focusing on silence-- "Conquered," "Unnecessary," "Hurricane Watch," and "The Logic of Silence"--relate to the concept of silence as expressed in "Approaching Nadá"?

VM: It has often seemed to me that the ultimate truth may only be expressed in symbol or in silence--either a High Mass or a Quaker Meeting for Worship. Silence has often meant to me the unexpressable, the ineffable in beauty, truth, whatever. For some reason I can't find "Resolve," but in "Conquered," "Unnecessary," and in "The Logic of Silence," silence means simply the absence of speech.

KH: "Resolve" is in *My Bones Being Wiser*. It begins with "I must go back to the small place,/to the swept place,/to the still place,/to the silence under the drip of the dew. . . ." You speak about "the crystal door of the air/hung on the hinge of the wind."

VM: "The silence under the drip of the dew" would mean the absence of all noise. But this physical silence symbolizes the ineffable.

KH: Why is silence such a focal theme for you? In saying *Wage War on Silence* did you mean that poetry is in conflict with silence, a means of countering silence? Is silence important to you because of your solitary lifestyle? What is the paradox silence best embodies? I was thinking of the possible relationship between silence and loneliness--the latter which you envision "like a small beast from the woods/made a pet" ("Heritage") in that it must be domesticated, tamed, turned from a loss into a gain. There must, of course, be a concomitant understanding that such domesticity of change is not permanently possible and that in each instance it must be challenged and conquered anew.

VM: I'm alone a good deal, but I wouldn't call my lifestyle solitary. There was a time a few years ago when I gave lots of parties. Poetry does that, it turns silence, in its negative aspects, from a loss to a gain. I suppose part of my focusing upon silence is the fact that I have a speech impediment and can't express myself as freely as I might.

KH: Why is loneliness so frequently imaged as an animal: "small dog dancing at my feet,/brown shadow of my loneliness. . ." ("The Calling of the Names");

"the gaunt black wolf/who crouches in some lair/of corner, cranny, shelf,/Ready to pounce and tear" ("Fait Accompli"); "let me recall/how many have waked up early and found loneliness waiting/like a small beast from the woods/made a pet,. . ." ("Heritage"); "I myself am that bird,/loneliness that silence" ("Origin"); "I think how most old maids'/affection for their pets is loneliness, . . ." ("Remembering Aunt Helen")?Or Loneliness is equated with clothing: "it's pelt like a mantle/ fallen upon them/from a vanishing form" ("Heritage"); "My lonely feet refuse,/Lightly, their heavy shoes" ("On Not Making a Retreat")? Do you see a parallel between time ("an angry little beast/clawing inside us, tearing us to shreds" ("Philosophy of Time")) and loneliness?

VM: I symbolize loneliness as a pet because animals are sometimes so wistful, so cut off from our concerns, at least dogs, and they often look as if they're trying to understand and be understood. If I anthropomorphize, I anthropomorphize! I've often longed to get rid of loneliness as easily as a cloak--in the past. It rarely bothers me now. I don't know as I see a parallel between time and loneliness.

KH: Speaking of time, "Time moving in us, not we in time" ("Philosophy of Time")--isn't that a little like the paradox that art does not reflect life but life reflects art? That inversion of/on reality?

VM: I think that "time moving in us, not we in time" refers to my belief that time is somehow a human invention, not real, or, more specifically, that time moves fast or slow (seems to, that is) according to our inner states.

KH: The Sun Has No History seems like a much more personal testament than early poetry volumes. What has been the impetus for a poetry that addresses specific events and people in the past? A coming to terms with life and death?

VM: Yes. Or maybe now that I am older, I grow more interested in my own personal history. Young people are not so interested. At least I wasn't. Now as I see my future diminishing I tend to look behind at my own past and that of my family. Questions occur to me that never did before, questions sometimes for which there are no answers, since those who could provide them are dead. But if a backward look now and then makes for poems, that is all to the good.

KH: Because "Hours leave no fingerprints/for sleuths of memory to trace" ("The Sun Has No History"), is it natural to depend on such symbols as cicadas to recall earlier times? (i.e., "Dry throat of summer rasping with cicadas--" ("Not Going Away Gift")? You have a number of references to cicadas throughout your poems ("Exercise in Remembering," "What the Cicada Says," "On Approaching My Birthday," "Toward the End," "Invocation," "Lullaby for My Mother," "Song for a Summer Afternoon," "Faintly and from Far Away"). Interestingly, two of these poems are for your mother. Does the cicada symbolize time passage ("drawing me back through the lost years"), grief ("their [cicadas] hidden harpsichords accompanying/her [your mother's] grief," and a world "where/pleasure and/melancholy merge" ("What the Cicada Says")? In other words, that which gave joy but is unretrievable because it is lost to the past? Does the cicada symbolize life ("happiness mixed with the herb of grief" ("To a Role Model")? The cicada reference from "High Noon" ("The cicadas' antiphonal choirs/one memory's and one desire's") suggests that cicadas can be equated with memory.

VM: Cicadas for me represent the essence of summer days--hot, sweaty, boring, but also pleasant and peaceful. I remember hearing them first when I was about five, lying in my maternal grandmother's porch swing. I suppose I would equate them with nostalgia, rather than memory. Of the two poems for my mother, the sonnet is

for my real mother, who died when I was a year old, the second for my stepmother, who died last August.
KH: To take this idea of time a little further. . . .Is there a contradiction set up between "Philosophy of Time" ("It is my heart, dear heart, that clocks my coming/toward you as it clocked your going from me,. . .") and "Unteachable" ("Heart has no history/ being born every minute/after yesterday did not happen")? If heart "clocks" someone's movement (approach/departure) in "Philosophy of Time," how can it exist without chronicling, making history as "Unteachable" suggests? Are the "pain" of "Philosophy of Time" and "Unteachable" one and the same? Why is the heart "illiterate"?
VM: There is a contradiction only if one assumes that a poet writes with a set of propositions always in mind. Some poets may. I don't. Not that I don't have an underlying view of life, but I'm not always true to it as a poet or as a human being. In "Unteachable" I was feeling that I don't learn from experience. That's why the heart is "illiterate," or, rather, the heart doesn't learn because it is illiterate. The pain is more generalized in "Unteachable." In "Philosophy of Time" it is the pain of separation.
KH: A more recent book, *Approaching Nada,* seems to depict less tangible symbols--distance, nothingness, faith (again), etc. Why are the individual poems of *Approaching Nada* untitled? Has this been criticized as seeming fragmented?
VM: "Approaching Nada" is a spiritual biography and is all one poem in five parts. I've seen only one review and that was entirely favorable.
KH: Do you see a parallel between the "ineffable" ("The poet like a mouse will scuttle/clean to the Border/of the ineffable,/then scurry back/with tidbits of the Vision") and the idea of approaching nada? Can it be equated with silence? Is there anything existential in

this concept?

VM: Yes, the Spanish mystics, St. Teresa, or at least St. John of the Cross, refer to God as Nada, as ineffable. Hindu mystics refer to the Ultimate reality as "Neti," "Not this." It can be equated with silence. What can you say about the ineffable?

KH: Can it be equated with the earlier quotation that "poetry is that which is unspeakable"? Doesn't this contain a basic paradox by definition? On one hand "ineffable" means indescribable, as in joy, or unspeakable, as in disgust. Is it an article of faith?

VM: When I say poetry says that which is ineffable (not "unspeakable," I hope! Somerset Maugham says, "The mystic sees the ineffable; the madman sees the unspeakable"), I'm using hyperbole as well as paradox. I mean that the poet never captures a meaning entirely in words. This is an article of a poetic credo.

KH: "Ideal retreat for poetry or prayer,/synonyms, ideally, for each other:/both have their dry runs, black nights of the soul. . ."("The Outsider"). Why, if it is, is poetry a retreat from the world? Wouldn't this depend on the kind of poetry one writes? For example, I don't think of war poetry (such as Denise Levertov's or Robert Bly's) or sexual identity poems (such as Adrienne Rich's, Olga Brouma's, or Audre Lorde's) as a retreat from the world. Their work is more a personal confrontation with the world. Don't you agree?

VM: In "The Outsider" I meant "retreat" as a place in which to write poetry or to pray. Since I regard poetry as a confrontation with the deepest self and prayer as a confrontation with God, I don't regard either one as a running away from the world.

KH: "My race guilt I shrug off/as too abstract a tribute for a friend" ("Elegy"). Could it also be--besides being too abstract--that you don't view poetry as an arena for conflicting polemics? That any ideology to which poetry aspires should be rooted as much in the spirit as in the flesh? Yet, "After Guyana" seems to suggest another possibility?

VM: Poetry can be an arena for conflicting polemics, but I think good poetry rarely is, simply because I believe Wordsworth had a point in calling poetry "emotion recollected in tranquility," and you can't be very tranquil when you're engaging in polemics. I'm not sure why "After Guyana" seems to suggest another possibility?

KH: "After Guyana" seems to be suggesting the conflicting polemics of good and evil. Added to this is the paradox and irony the words (in this poem) themselves convey. In calling Evil "death's other face" aren't you negating the idea of Heaven (as opposed to Hell) as a place of everlasting happiness and goodness?

VM: No, death is the ultimate human limitation. St. Paul speaks of death as "the last enemy." What may come *after* death is another matter.

KH: "All their sinister/innocence like the garment/with no seam but Christ's blood" ("Germany, 1976"). Were you speaking to the memory of Nazi Germany in the image of sinister? Why "innocence"? Do you see a parallel between "Germany, 1976" and "Age of Aquarius, Age of Assassins," in what is being said about the Jews and the Nazis: guilt, responsibility, atonement?

VM: Yes, I visited the "Eagles Nest," which has been turned into a restaurant and a tourist site. Men in Alpine costumes were singing and dancing. Such innocence, real or assumed, is sinister, because it may allow a like evil and terror to happen again. Yes, I did see a parallel between the Nazis and the situation in "Age of Aquarius, Age of Assassins."

KH: Why in *Approaching Nada* did you say: "One might become Quaker/in this aztec land/where Christ is mostly Catholic. . ."? Why "mostly Catholic"?

VM: Approaching Nada II describes a desert setting in Arizona, suggesting the Spanish influence. Hence, "mostly Catholic."

KH: Is "The Protestant Cemetery in Florence" for Elizabeth Barrett Browning? Did her life and death occasion this poem? What does her epitath "Nothing is final. Only this." mean in terms of your own life? In terms of a preoccupation with death?

VM: Yes. After I visited England and Florence where EBB is buried, I read a biography of her. I was shocked to learn that she took opium until her death. I'd assumed that marriage had solved all her problems. Of course, that couldn't have been true. Our earthly problems go on, mine, yours, and everybody's, till they carry us out feet first.

KH: In what way is poetry sanctifying? Does the secret of this lie in the unanswered question asked in "Posthumous Letter to Thomas Merton"? Does this in any way contradict what you've said in "Requiem for Some Poets" that "Poetry's no gift of the Holy Ghost--"? Would you elaborate on what you've called poetry's "trinitarian function: creative, redemptive, and sanctifying." In the years since you've written *Wage War on silence*, would you add any other qualities or functions to this list?

VM: Poetry can be said to be sanctifying in the sense that it confers order on chaotic emotions and experience. Maybe that forms part of the answer to the question in "Posthumous Letter," but I was really thinking of "suffers" in general. Sure it contradicts what I've said in "Requiem for Some Poets" in a sense. But in that poem I was thinking of all the poets who have committed suicide and wondering whether poetry wasn't a dangerous gift after all. Poetry is a way of ordering life, but it's also often a sign of a nature extraordinarily sensitive to pain--as well, of course, as to joy.

Poetry is creative in that it makes an artifact where none was before, only a mass of thoughts and emotions and sensations; it is redemptive, since it makes art out

of non-art, something of beauty and value; it is sanctifying in that it confers order upon chaos. These three
functions are one. Poetry helps to sensitize the reader.
It should also sensitize the reader, specifically, to language. The sheer ability to create expands and enlarges
the personality. I'm sure there are a myriad of other
functions and qualities which haven't occurred to me.
KH: Could you explain what you meant in saying:
"Every poet knows/what the saint knows:/that every
new day is/to retake the frontier of one's name" (*Approaching Nada*)? How does this relate to what you've
said elsewhere in *Approaching Nada* (IV) about poets,
mystics and saints or "Although I wander/down hallways of my body, ghost/ prowling passages of my
blood/to my most hidden corners,still/I know my name"
(*Approaching Nada*)? Is this related to what you've said
elsewhere ("Second Rate") about saints' wounds being
honored ("But delegates us sinners/His cold Assistant,
Time")? Do you feel that these images of the spiritual
life further serve as a connective between poetry and
prayer elsewhere?
VM: Somebody had commented that Robert Lowell could
afford to write some bad poems since he had written so
many good ones. In writing "An Essay in Criticism By
Way of Rebuttal" I was refuting this idea and saying
that in every poem one has to strive for excellence. In
Approaching Nada I'm saying that the poet has his/her
kind of heroism as well as the saint. In the last section
of *Approaching Nada* I'm saying that a saint might find
balm in prayer, whereas the rest of us might have to let
the pain wear off. I'm less sure about that dichotomy
now. But if a metaphor is apt, does it have to be
absolutely true? After all, who can say what a saint is?
KH: That's true--they vary from Joan of Arc to T.S.
Eliot's Celia Coplestone (*The Cocktail Party*).To continue
with *Approaching Nada*. . .would you elaborate on what
occasioned "Abbe Bremond. . ." Part IV.

VM: The Abbe Bremond (Henri was his first name, I think) said in his treatise *Priere et Poesie* that the poet is a *mystique manque*. Whereas the mystic crossed over the line where he/she could speak of the vision or of communion with God, the poet comes back while he/she still can speak of his/hers. This always seemed to be a nice idea. The poet isn't necessarily a saint (God knows I'm not), but the poet still has a lonely commitment, a rigorous discipline.

KH: Isn't this true for any artistic discipline? Does the question of sainthood with respect to poetry center on the fact of redemption? Can you think of any poets who have become saints?

VM: Poetry can redeem experience from oblivion or from chaos. John of the Cross was canonized as a saint. I can't offhand think of anybody else canonized. And I don't know how we can point to some one and say, "He/she's a saint."

KH: How do you feel about reviewers saying that *If I Could Sleep Deeply Enough* is more "honest" than your earlier work? (i.e., Susan Wood in *Houston Chronicle*, December 15, 1974)?

VM: I was as honest as I knew how to be in writing all my poems. Most critics seem to think that any expression of religious faith is dishonest.

KH: Why do you think that is? Because most critics tend to intellectualize and refuse to base their convictions on something they interpret to be as tenuous as faith?

VM: No, because we live in a post-Christian, post-religious era. No doubt most critics and other poets consider my religiousness at best an exotic hobby, at worst a disease.

KH: Death is a frequent image in your poems. Would you say that in the face of inevitable death, there is the opportunity for redemptive love? Is this what poetry "as an act of love" makes possible?

VM: As a Christian I have to say that redemptive love is possible even in the face of inevitable death. Basically, God's grace makes this possible. Admittedly, I don't always feel like this and so not all of my poetry sounds like this.

KH: Why is Death "the dark nurse"? Why "nurse"? Is there any relationship between this image and an image in "On Opening One Eye" "--from night, the nurse who, dark and faceless"?

VM: One might say that Death is the "dark nurse" that puts us all to bed. In "On Opening One Eye" the nurse is sleep.

KH: In "Warning to Thomas Wolfe," what did you mean in saying "You scorned their town of liars./Now they are only notarizing your word."?

VM: I was thinking of the commemorative celebration Wolfe's hometown held for him--the same hometown outraged by his novel *You Can't Go Home Again*. Their belated praise, after he was dead and famous, seemed an exercise in hypocrisy.

KH: Would you elaborate on "I guess/we all of us take our chances who play/Russian-roulette with words" ("Requiem for Some Poets"). How is poetry risk-taking? I assume from your poem that Thomas Chatterton committed suicide? Can you tell me something about the circumstances?

VM: I was referring to the prevalence of suicide among modern poets and musing whether poetry might be a risky occupation. Of course, I wasn't entirely serious. Thomas Chatterton, a young poet in the seventeeth century took poison, and died because he was starving to death. His landlady invited him to supper, but, too proud to accept, he committed suicide instead.

KH: Was this information derived from a biography of his life?

VM: Louis Untermeyer edited an anthology of English and American poets that had a running commentary on their lives. I got the information from that source.

KH: Has poetry ever seemed a risky occupation for you personally?

VM: No, though sometimes I've felt that many people probably consider it a "useless" occupation for a "useless," i.e., handicapped person.

KH: We've discussed poetry as risk-taking. . . .Do you think it's a matter of gender as well? How do you respond to the ALA *Booklist's* review (3/15/64) statement that *My Bones Being Wiser* are "intensely feminine poems in tone and theme yet usually shaped with a masculine spareness and economy"? Do you see this masculine/feminine rift or union in your work? Is it the legacy of earlier influences?

VM: I don't think of poetry as a matter of gender. I don't consider myself a feminist poet, because, although certainly I am pro-ERA, frankly, as a handicapped individual I have been put down by as many women as men, so somehow I feel a little left out of the concerns of women. Then, too, I'm excluded more because of my handicap than because of my gender. I know my position isn't totally justified, but that's how I feel.

I'm sure whoever made that statement would say "Ah ha!" if they knew that my father always made me cut excess verbiage from my school themes. But I don't think sparseness and economy is either masculine or feminine. I think people often see a masculine/feminine rift in a lot of places where there is none.

KH: We've discussed your poetry now at some length. . . .I understand that you write fiction as well. Can you tell me something about the collection of short stories I've been told you're compiling? Themes, characters, or the circumstances and/or events of a particular story?

VM: I'm not compiling any short stories. I've written about a dozen, but haven't written any in over ten years. A few have been published. Usually they've been based on incidents in my childhood. I've also written some plays. None have been performed. Only one may have merit. I've also thought of writing a novel, but probably I won't.

KH: Why has childhood provided you with the most usable or compelling material for fiction? Have any of your plays been published? What playwrights have been models for you? What would stop you from writing a novel?

VM: A great many fiction writers have drawn upon their childhood. That's when our emotional habits are formed for better or for worse. As I said, none of my plays have been produced. I wrote them willy-nilly without thinking of any models. Your very question probably dignifies my playwriting more than it deserves. I did write one chapter of a novel once. Another time I thought of making a short story the basis of a novel and added several incidents. Fear that I couldn't sustain the effort and material and, perhaps, sheer laziness are what stop me from writing a novel.

KH: Has there been a particularly memorable moment as a poet? In your career in writing?

VM: I guess my firsts were memorable--my first published poem in *The Hopkins Review* and my first book, *Adam's Footprint*.

KH: What have been some of the advantages in living out of the mainstream of poetry? By this I mean not living in New York City or being surrounded by other poets? Not being a regular attender of workshops or a resident of writing colonies (MacDowell, Yaddo, Blythewold, etc.)?

VM: Not many advantages--except maybe that being out of the mainstream keeps one from becoming inbred and pompous. I love poetry, but it would bore me to death to think of nothing *except* poetry.

Allowing for Such Talk

PAUL CHRISTENSEN

For over thirty years Vassar Miller has been composing poems and sorting them into various collections; nine books of poetry have appeared in that time. Though she has drawn an appreciative audience to her, there has been little serious criticism of her writing. Fellow poets certainly admire her, but even so watchful a guardian of Texas poets as Dave Oliphant has been more vigilant and supportive of the work of William Barney and others than he has of Vassar Miller. In *On a High Horse: Views Mostly of Latin American & Texas Poetry*, Oliphant counted Miller among William Barney and William Burford as a "first generation" of Texas poets, whose "poetry (is) of high seriousness and is marked by linguistic power and a mastery of traditional forms." (1) Later in his essay "Generations of Poets," he remarked that Miller's style of the 1960s was influenced by "the confessionalists Sylvia Plath and Robert Lowell," for whom Oliphant has little enthusiasm; but he is quick to stress that all three poets "creat[ed] their styles and ideas independently, and that either they preceded certain trends in the '60s or carried on an existing tradition after a wholly regional manner." (2) Oliphant published Miller's poetry in several of his anthologies, in *The New Breed* (1973) and again in *Washing the Cow's Skull* (1981), but his scrupulous honesty compelled him to admit that Miller is more like the invading "emigre" poets, with whom she is frequently associated, than she is like the native bards. She has not been "concerned with region," which to Oliphant is the principal subject matter of Texas poetry. He has shown an unswerving devotion to a core of

native writers who have made regional life in Texas
their chief concern. In these asides, Oliphant thus explains why he has not been one of her stauncher
supporters.

But the irony is, Miller has been passed over by
critics of national literature *because* of her regional
tendencies. She has found herself in the middle of the
main extremes of literary taste: she is neither broad in
her grasp of politics and social issues nor local or literal
in her sense of belonging. For that reason she has
eluded the attention of critics for many years, and would
have continued eluding them had not Larry McMurtry
brought her to sudden notice in his scathing address to
an audience at the Fort Worth Art Museum in 1981,
"Ever a Bridegroom: Reflections on the Failure of Texas
Literature" (3) Having castigated both the living and the
dead of Texas literature for failing to write estimable
poetry and fiction, McMurtry reserved the close of his
remarks to "reverse my thrust and pay tribute. . .to
the one Texas writer for whose work I have an unequivocal admiration: that is, Vassar Miller." (4) Though his
praise for Miller is indeed unequivocal, the example of
Miller as the one unspoiled achiever says less about
Miller's poetry than it does of McMurtry's powers of
homily. Her virtues are that she works "in the hardest
form--the lyric poem." where she has achieved "excellence: the product of a high gift wedded to long-sus-
tained and exceedingly rigorous application." Her work
is "hard-won, high, intelligent, felt, finished, profound." (5) Some twelve of her poems, McMurtry says
tauntingly, will "outlast all the books mentioned in this
essay, plus the 50 on A.C. Greene's list as well." (6) It
would not have been lost upon his stunned audience
that the one figure for whom he reserved praise is a
religious writer, whose work had all been in the least
marketable form of writing, the "lyric poem."

Though their attitudes toward Miller's work may be

opposite, Oliphant and McMurtry both admire her evident craftsmanship and have used similar language to
praise it: "high-seriousness," "hard-won, high, intelligent, profound." And indeed it does not take a reader
long to realize that her poetry is full of lucid phrases
and cleanly organized stanzas of argument. Her poems
have a worked surface in which rime scheme has been
rigorously tuned and sustained; her techniques are not
those of surprise and finesse, but of anticipated fulfill-
ment of pattern and function. The poems are rounded
off, fitted together, sturdily joined--like that of good
cabinet making. The hesitations of voice in her best
poems have been removed, to leave behind a flow of
precise, unwavering declaration, like that of Emily Dickinson, whose style Miller's poetry most often resembles:

> Death we can manage,
> mincing along
> bearing our black bows of condolence.
>
> But this our mind
> can scarcely handle,
> too heavy even for our tongues.
>
> lacking decorum
> to shape this rawness
> which must make up its own words.
> "Improvisation" (SSC, p. 34)

Silence and the unknown appealed to both Dickinson
and Miller. Many of Dickinson's poems are about falling
through the final "plank" of reason into uknown voids
of experience, to "finish knowing then," or to discover
that "Much madness is divinest Sense." She describes
herself as "the little tippler," and seems to drift near
the edge of consciousness for her subject matter. Indeed, armed with the limpid grammar of neoclassical

prose and the aggressive rhythms of Charles Wesley's hymns, Dickinson felt sufficiently protected to explore the dark fringes of rational life. Neoclassical English, on which her and Miller's lyric simplicity are based, is a powerful instrument for articulating dilemmas and emotional crises; its roots are in Elizabethan prose, but the Puritans had pruned back the lavish wordplay of Shakesspear, Lyly, and Donne to create a modest, though flexible medium in which to sort out the affairs of newly urbanized English life. Its practicality and aggressive syntax enabled Addison, Steele, Johnson and Pope to teach their countrymen how to live well in a city. Its simplicity and sober logic were effective means for a woman writing in Puritan New England, as it awoke to the modern era.

Coming more than a century later, Miller's situation is less bleak, perhaps; though even here, one must pause at some intriguing parallels between the two writers. Cerebral palsy left Miller in relative isolation; society might well seem as intimidating to her as it did to Dickinson, in its intolerance of physical debility. But the closest parallel is that both women witnessed profound shifts in their regional cultures, as rural life gave way to urban civilization. Though attracted to its novelty and potential freedom, each had been formed in the image of the old order and could not escape the pattern of her life to participate in the new. Their powerful energies were thwarted and driven to a subliminal level of lyric self-analysis and reverie, to indulge an imaginary plane of experience that reflected the real one outside. From their private vantages, they could cooly anatomize events as they unfolded, and perceive the dangers as well as the pleasures of their tumultuous eras. Their resilience partly derived from faith in strong men, who they found in their fathers, in potential lovers, and certainly in religion itself, with its powerful ministers and patriarchal deities. Their worship conflated sexual and spiritual needs, and satisfied longings for a paternal authority in their lives.

In the interim of a century or more, it is possible to see in Dickinson's work a profound reflection of region and local character. Her miniature lyrics resound with the thumping meters of Sunday service hymn-sings; her common sense logic is one with the Puritan merchant's thought; her fascination with an "outside" world of sensations and natural phenomena was shared by all her countrymen and is in thin disguise a "frontier" beckoning her. Her primary subject, pain, was the danger otherwise missing in her life; it was the language of the body, a terrain steeped in pagan lore and myth, and haunted with the mystery of death and renewal.

It remains to see how the clipped measures and the fervid religious yearnings of Miller's work reflect the nature of the Southwest, and voice the local situation of a woman writing in Houston about her life at mid-century, just as Texas was waking from the torpors of its long neglect as a remote outpost of the U.S. From her vantage in the 1950s, she watched the transformation of Texas from rural to urban culture, and though she disapproved of much of the hubbub and raucous wheeling and dealing, in which her father played a significant part, her observations have the same ring of truth as do Lexie Dean Robertson's poems in *Boom Town*, which chronicled the days of the wild catters further west. Though never explicit, Miller's poems hint at the emergence and spread of Houston as the business center of post-war Texas.

Even so, the "frontier" was very much a lingering presence of Texas life; as it receded into memory, its pasing was loudly lamented in popular music, western painting, folkloric studies, and in fashion. The dying out of the old ways was met with sentimentality and protestation, usually aimed at the encroachments of the city, with its levelling of such cherished ideals as self-reliance, independence, freedom to live apart. The ranch was a compact symbol of American transcendentalist notions; a unit of individual worth, a sovereign principality of the ordinary soul.

These thoughts circulated in Miller's earliest poetry and gave her imagery and metaphors a certain tanginess of Southwestern life. Even her childhood play bore the memory of pioneer hunters, as she stamped her foot down on "round plump bugs" to "make them stop,"

> My bantam brawn could turn them back.
> My crooked step wrenched straight to kill
> Live pods that then screwed tight and still.
> > "Adam's Footprint," (*SNP*, p. 13)

Wilderness is a pure thing among dilute and corrupted human values; to name it was sufficient to draw upon those latent assumptions.

> Deer and bear we used to stalk,
> We would spend our dying pains
> Nestling you with mouse and hawk
> Near our warmth until it wanes.

> . . .Loathed no longer, learn your worth,
> Toad and lizard, snail and eel--
> Remnants of a living earth
> Cancelled by a world of steel,
> Whose miasmic glitter dances
> Over beast's and man's sick gaze. . . .
> > "Love Song for the Future," (*SNP*, p. 28)

Wilderness is many things to Miller, but chiefly it signifies fertility and innocence. It is the "womb's dense grove," a thing near death, since it is in jeopardy, and therefore the "whir of wings. . .called from the dusk of death"; love is "elusive like the wind," "fugitive like air," a vitalizing breath out of nature. "Loneliness is "a small beast from the woods/made a pet,"

> which, when it grew up,
> for all that they had coaxed it with words
> / or with work,
> would turn wild again
> and tear them

> though it had worn
> the shape of their loves. And though they
> / might kill it, they wore
> its pelt like a mantle
> fallen upon them

> from a vanishing form. . . .
> "Heritage," (*SNP*, p. 40-41)

Nature is the transcendent thing, the collective unconsciousness in many of her poems:

> The leaves blow speaking
> green, lithe words
> in no man's language.

> . . .the leaves
> breathe through me all men's
> in no man's language.
> "Precision," (*SNP*, p. 42)

It is, in fact, something asleep, below language and outside the range of logical category or rational grasp; it is the edenic setting of love, "Where flesh and spirit dance,/Shadowing, bound yet free." Lovers take the form of "two arrows bound together/wounding no one" in "Regret." (*SNP*, p. 49) It is the opposite of "the desert of the day," though she will describe urban monotony as "marshes" and "flatlands of finitude," where a desultory waking life plods on mechanically. Outside nature is a realm of things and ways of life that belong to adulthood, which Miller usually treats as a negative state, except for the sexuality that is its one link to nature. Adulthood is rationality, a conscious state of defense and aggression, an outlook altogether destructive and manipulative, violently opposed to the will in other things:

> My flesh is
> the shadow of pride
> cast by my bones
> at whose core lies cradled a child tender
> and terrible. . . .
> "My Bones Being Wiser," (*SNP*, p. 61)

The bones are rooted in a fragment of wilderness in her own unconscious, "beneath the dark waters of my blood, . . .huddled together, rubbing themselves," to become later the "bundle of faggots/ready for burning." Thus, they form a sort of cane break in which the infant soul is nurtured, though the mind elsewhere lives on in the adult world of indifference and scepticism. The bones are wiser because they live in nature, "the womb's dense grove," apart from "the swirling sand dunes" of ordinary consciousness. "O Lord," begins De Profundis," defend me when I go/Through the dark in daylight," "when snowfalls of words melt in/deserts of my deafness."

In a recent poem, "Seasonal Change," she describes her imaginal life in terms of a frontier between adult urbanity and primal nature: "I have built a home/On my edge of existence," having lived too long in "The temperate climate of unconcern." (*SSC*, p. 33) In another recent poem, the argument against the quotidian world of consciousness is made very pungently:

> Light, whose limping whisper was thought,
> snagged upon inertia,
> knotting into lumps.
>
> "Fall," (SSC, p. 49)

Light "descending from self-contemplation" became a sort of heavy film over the senses, "matted to matter, clotted to shape." Adulthood and its concommitant residence, the city, are the subject of "Whitewash of Houston," a breathless tirade on the city as a defiled mother (as in metro: mater, polis: city) "driving all her children dumb/down the long chute of death and safely home?" (*SSC*, p. 20) In Part II, the "mother" is remembered in the pre-war days of smalltown Houston, where the imagery shifts to plenitude and fertility, "her apron smelling of summer." A similar treatment of the city appears in "In Quiet Neighborhoods":

> Now that watch fires are out, monsters tormented,
> murdered, lassoed, confined to dull extinctions,
> caught on our barbed wire kindness, the wild moon
> Diana no longer, merely rock admired
> by men who skim its surface, lumbering ghosts
> found more miraculous than myth or fable--
> no sheep may safely graze our savage lawns.
>
> (SSC, p. 46)

For nine stanzas, this poem rebukes the "feast of lights" that "forbids the famished from our tight doors," locked against a night in which "the darkness swells with grace and judgment."

In these and many other poems, the polarity between the city as corrupt experience and loss of vision, nature as innocence and fertile unconscious, would suggest that Miller is saying the very things McMurtry roundly denounces in other writers in Texas literature. As he remarked in "Ever a Bridegroom,"

. . .virtually the whole of modern literature has been a city literature. From the time of Baudelaire and James, the dense, intricate social networks that cities create have stimulated artists and sustained them. No reason it should be any different in Texas, since we now have at least one or two cities which offer the competitions of manners upon which the modern novel feeds. [But] where has this experience gone? Where are the novels, stories, poems, and plays that ought to be using it? Why are there still cows to be milked and chickens to be fed in every other Texas book that comes along? When is enough going to be allowed to be enough? (7)

As if to rebut all this, Miller's poem "Liebstod" opens,

If I could merge myself into the country
Of trees and shrubs and where the air flows pure
Over my head, so battered by the sentry
of fixed identity,. . .
But steel-gilt buildings, hidden less each mile,
Sprout blooming pallid hues of the horizon,
Tall toadstools delicate with dawn--and poison.

(SSC, p. 66)

McMurtry's essay is interesting not for its damning and small praise, but for its unwitting confrontation with the most basic issue of Texas writing: its passion for nature and rural life to the exclusion of nearly everything else. (8) In this, Miller would appear to be the more sure and correct of her position as a writer, having continued to damn the city and praise agrestic values, and to encrust her arguments with symbols of primal nature. McMurtry appears to fumble at this question, and turns against his own readers as retrograde in their tastes and expectations of literature. "Part of the trouble I am afraid, lies with Texas readers, who, if my experience is any indication, remain actively hostile to the mere idea of urban fiction." (9) Artists who succumb to their demands show "intellectual laziness." "The result," McMurtry concludes, "is a limited, shallow, self-repetitious literature which has so far failed completely to do justice to the complexities of life in the state."(10)

But all of Miller's poetry would suggest that the subjects of nature and of rural life were, in fact, a direct response to the city, though in ways less demonstratively overt than McMurtry recommends. Her poems are in line with the major post-romantic tradition in rejecting industrial urban culture, and in finding vitality and renewal only in those things belonging to an undefined prior world. Her equation of nature with the unconscious, with primal instincts, with freedom of emotion has a long heritage going back to Blake, Coleridge, and Wordsworth; its message goes to the very heart of Southwestern culture: for it is almost entirely predicated upon a mystic vision of nature and the old ways as the source of youth and strength. Debility and corruption lay in human realms of the city, of civilization, of commerce and competition; the ideal of purity is a young man or woman raised close to nature, who knows self-reliance in a primal setting, and who thinks like an animal, with cunning, shrewdness, and keen survival strategy. The "city" stands for the thinning of blood race; the separation of man from nature withers youth and vitality; like the myth of Antaeus, whose mother was earth and whose touch revived his powers, man is strong only in the presence of natural things, and is vitiated by their absence. The "tender-foot," "green horn," "Easterner" and "city slicker," the man in "three-piece suit," the dandy, are all images of the dessication of urban life, the diminished powers of the human psyche when sequestered in artificiality. These caricatures populate the satiric fiction of the Southwestern literature from Mark Twain to the present.

Miller's canon is steeped in these prejudices and idealizations common to Southwestern art and thought. Indeed, her views of the city are reinforced by much of popular culture, particularly western music, with its frequent laments at the loss of rural custom. Though the image of cowboy has long been cheapened and exploited by the nostalgia merchants, beneath the tawdriness of the "urban cowboy" and the dance halls, the dude ranches and western wear outfitters is a heart-felt conviction that one is rejuvenated by symbols of old west days, that a grain of youth is imparted to the person who retains some small part of its memory. But it is the *youth* longed for that makes these fragments of the western past cohere to express a regional ethos; there is thus a richly developed myth of youth invested in the image of pioneering on the western plains, of living apart on small holdings, of driving cattle and camping in the wilds. As cities spread, they compelled a more emphatic expression of this myth--as a means of coping with, of accepting the losses and changes that accompany the transformation of Southwestern life. The almost universal preoccupation of writers and artists with the passing of the old ways, notably in the strong dramatic studies of it by Sam Shepard, involves far more than artists bending to the will of their audience. Rather, in marking this passage artists not only had a compelling subject matter but a pretext for exploring a psychological landscape, a mythic reality of place. The dissolution of nature in everyday life is a commentary on aging and an exploration of death itself. The city's inorganic symmetry and amorality are features of a counter-mythology of age and experience. Thus, the "urban cowboy" is a figure who has joined the ends of paradox in himself, and his decadent and erotic qualities are aspects of his *ruined* youth, his squandered energies.

Miller's poetry ignores obvious Southwestern symbolism and goes to the heart of the issue behind it to youth itself. Freedom and creativity are most deeply felt when she can impersonate the thought or voice of a child, when she can revivify a memory of her childhood and relive it lyrically. The "child" in her poetry is the most insistent of her varied repertoire of voices. But child is a ubiquitous term from the very beginning: "Once as a child I loved to hop. . ." and so on through the years. Her affectionate addresses to her father reinforce the persona of the child: "to my comfort as my father's stir/In sleep once solaced my child's heart."

> . . .you cheat me of my anger
> with your gentleness,
> making my thoughts children
> that sit around you,
> flowers wilting and waiting
> the dews of your attention.
>
> "Conquered," (*SNP*, p.34)

Hence, the bones "at whose core lies cradled a child tender and terrible," and the merry child's voice in "And,"

> when poems sprouted out of my skin
> that slap-happy time when I dreamed love growing
> on trees money doesn't
>
> (*SNP*, p. 82)

In "Cycle," one has the theme of rejuvenation pure and simple:

> Love never went
>
> more naked to bed than when

my body shrugs off
logic's gold sheath

in the black irrational. . . .

(*SNP*, p. 88)

Youth returns in "Lying in Bed Late," when

I keep the darkness locked behind my lashes
To seed my flesh with sleep,
                / my head with dreams,
Pulsing to melody within my blood,
Making my stiff bones burgeon
                / like green branches.

(*NSP*, p. 91)

In "Insomniac's Prayer," "dreams jump out of my
skull/like pictures in a child's pop-up book." (*SNP*, p.90)
In "Transmogrification," renewal lay in becoming a
simple thing of nature:

I am rooted
into rocks that lie
in cool absolutes of sleep.

I stare puzzling
over the difference
between my feet and this earth.

(*SNP*, p. 109)

"I grow from my poems/in a green world" she writes
in "Raison D'Etre." Poetry and youth are one medium
in her work; to think in poetry is to return to youth; the
natural state of childhood is that pre-logical stage of
human awareness where purest freedom and daring
exist, but for the last time. The awakening to this
freedom occurs in a mythic paradigm of the father

bringing home a typewriter, in "Subterfuge,"

bearing it in his arms like an awkward bouquet

for his spastic child who sits down
on the floor, one knee on the frame
of the typewriter, and holding her left wrist

with her right hand. . . .

(*SNP*, p. 131)

Therefore, "wild child" is her elemental equivalent of "cowboy," with whom "we shoo death away." The child's realm is always furnished with a mythic tiger, a luxurious forest, and other archetypal symbolism to suggest nascent identity at some distant edge of civilization. In "Summation," there is a poignant description of aging:

loneliness
being the dew that melts
in solitude's sun,
since I have discovered
the court of my childhood
burned down, the halls of its
approval collapsed, and
have come home to myself
here in my homemade world.

(*SNP*, p. 139)

The equivalence of poetry with youth is summed up in "When the Living Is Easy," where she notes "the poem is outside me, . . .like a child tugging me out of my sleep." (*SNP*, p. 151) Of death, Miller writes in "Prayer to My Muse,"

I'm not too sorry,

longing to be back
coiled in my wombworld,

too smug and small, I know,
no wider than my bed
where no one sleeps but me.

(*SNP*, p. 157)

The emphasis on religion in Miller's poetry has
deterred some readers from a full appreciation of her
work. But its themes and subjects are inextricably bound
to her vision, and to dismiss it as doxology is to
misjudge the complexity of her thought, or the ranges of
her sensuality. Close readings of her meditations would
reveal an eccentric, even problematic relation to Christian belief. Miller's faith, like that of other artists of
strong belief, is profoundly emotional and creative, a-
gain, like Emily Dickinson's, who once wryly asserted,

Some keep the Sabbath going to Church--
I keep it, staying at Home--
With a Bobolink for a Chorister--
And an Orchard for a Dome--

and like Flannery O'Conner's, with whom Miller also
identifies herself. (Cf. "Affinity," *SSC*, p. 37) Her personal tradition of writers includes Thomas Merton, Teresa of Avila, and E.B. Browning; there are tributes and
dedications to Mary Magdalene, the Virgin Mary, Joan
of Arc on the one hand, and to Helen Keller, Anne
Sexton, Marianne Moore, and even Sophie Tucker on
the other. It would stretch things to say there is a
common denominator here, except for the obvious one of
all having powers to move others by their convictions
and talents. But such a tradition suggests the idiosyn-
cratic nature of her attitude and affections; her faith is
neither institutional nor casual, but a root of her

esthetic.

One aspect of her faith allows her to admit to a rote creed, a reductive and simple faith that is ironically literal in its pleadings, as in "Morning Person," (*SSC*, p. 29) which opens, "God, best at making in the morning, tossed/stars and planets, singing and dancing," etc. It is a child-like voice of belief, but it holds a clue to her other uses of religion. In "Exorcism," Miller makes one of her habitual connections between her father and religion:

> Father, glum ghost of Christmas Past,
> if you are anywhere around,
> I hope you are propitiated,
> old Christmas-hater!
>
> (*SSC*, p. 40)

The identification of parent with diety occurs whenever she enters her child-persona, where innocence of mind permits her to voice all manner of thought, especially her sexual longings. Combining hints of incestuous devotion with religious ecstasy, the tissue of these impressions is of an uncensored craving for love voiced in religious context:

> My tears at Silent Night smoke upward,
> orgasmic shivers
>
> along the spine of Midnight Mass
>
> (*SSC*, p. 40)

"Rest, rest" she tells her father, "ghost, child's god." Christ and her father are sometimes interchangeable suitors in her dreamscapes, and redemption can sometimes be confounded with rape, seduction, with "the dream of being broken into"

--come, Savior of
us, the ungentle, Holy Thief of night!

(*SSC*, p. 47)

Her father is "a second sun," and "Light," in the next
poem, is "God's pseudonymn,/ground from the guts of
sun." Even Eucharist bears sexual connotation; it is a
primal act, the taking of a divine lover. The usual
decorum attendant upon communion "would distract/
From this resplendence of the naked act." ("Dining
Room Eucharist," (*SSC*, p. 52) The "Mystery" of Christian revelation is "over our heads and hearts," she
writes in "The Inescapable Day," "like a child's
pajamas."

Faith is a venue back to youth; its figures and prin-
cipals form a landscape coterminous with the memory of
childhood; to enter one is to enter the other, where she
is blamelessly whole and primitive. In an impressive
sonnet sequence that closes *Struggling to Swim on
Concrete*, entitled "Love's Bitten Tongue," she remarks
on this feature in her faith:

Of praying may (in mercy become prayer)
My backward journey be--Christ, teach me this!
This trek begun and left when, hope to spare
I saw ahead a new metropolis
All burnished brightly with an innocence
Now peeled the same as paint from ancient houses

(*SSC*, p. 67)

Religions "backward journey" is psychological, a descent to the borders of preconsciousness, where holistic
thought is once more possible. Religion is an allied
function of mind, a voice out of the same faculty from
whence childhood achieves its vision of the world;hence,
the panoply of authoritative male deities who crowd her
thought as she voices, in child-like devotion, her urges

and desires to become one with them "As His old
daughter toddles safely home to God." Though religious
eroticism is nothing new to poetry, Miller's devotions
capture the polymorphous eroticism of adolescence, one
of the buried levels of religious ecstasy:

> Here where these white-headed trees
> blanched by the cold desert sun
> open upon rosy rock
> nippled and cocked toward the sky
> stabbing my eye with its gaze.
>
> "Approaching Nada," (*SNP*, p. 121)

In Sonnet 22 of "Love's Bitten Tongue," her frankness
is keen and earthy:

> So You have opened me to woe and wonder
> Much sharper than woe, far keener than pain
> Pitching the techniques of thought that
> / might pander
> To the gimmicks of mind, but split open mine
> That prays, "What shall I do, Jesus?
> / How deal
> With those flesh-splitting throbs, pain,
> / dread, rapture
> Which rupture my being drooping and dull
> To the literal Word, ecstatic scripture?"
>
> (*SSC*, p. 77)

Though Miller has several times changed churches,
she has stayed within the Protestant faith, which is
itself a bond with her region. The Protestant denom-
inations swept over Texas even before it separated from
Mexico. Protestantism broke the Spanish Catholic strong-
hold on the region, and interrupted a long reign of
medieval absolutism and aristocratic social control. The
evangelical churches that first penetrated the territory

were mobile, autonomous, and appealed to the free-thinking pioneers. The earliest congregations were thus in germ the first townships, villages, social units on the empty landscape. Religion is thus profoundly wedded to the rural past of the state; the revival of Christian religion since World War II goes hand-in-hand with renewed interest in early Southwestern life. Religion and the old ways possess the same attractions to the urban Texan: through faith, one literally revives the past and the youth that clings to its memory. The very term "reborn" suggest this rejuvenating them in Southern and Southwestern religion. The modern church, though vastly different in style and attitude from its rural antecedents, can still recreate the village atmosphere of early Texas thorugh church suppers, socials, baptisms, and other unifying events.

For Miller and for many others, religion is a "backward journey" to a mythic landscape. Miller's vision of faith is wider and more daring than that of the ordinary believer's; but she has not departed from the concept which all share alike: that in religion, one makes the descent to innocence and youth, and submits willingly to the drama of a Sunday service, to being a child again within a congregation, as a minister assumes the role of fatherly advisor to his flock. She enriched the vision by adding to it the rest of the pristine landscape of adolescence that Henri Rousseau, Blake, and Wordsworth earlier depicted, and that Dickinson voiced:

> "We'll talk all night until we swoon away,"
> / you promised.
> friend of my innocence, and of no more
> / than that,
> the only rule allowing for such talk.
>
> (*SSC*, p. 51)

Miller is both bound to her own region and transcends it; she shares the fears and prejudices of her countrymen, and her artistry bears the same careful craftsmanship to be found in country quilts and ranch-house carpentry. But there is a knowing sophistication in her use of her materials; she orders them with a wise simplicity and a grasp of their philosophical importance. She among those poets who have been posted throughout history at the border between country ways and the rise of cities; her themes are all the losses involved in change, and of how one copes with them.

Crying Out: Aloneness and Faith in the Poetry of Vassar Miller

KENNETH MACLEAN

Perry Miller's *Errand into the Wilderness* used the phrase initially: pioneers of the human self, Americans found themselves spiritually outside of time and history, he said, and thereby, "alone with America." (1) Like Alexis De Tocqueville's assertion that the poets of democracy would "stand aloof," and "in the presence of Nature and of God," write almost solely of Man himself, (2) this sort of prophetic generalization has become substantially descriptive of American poetic consciousness. And for those who wish to be orthodoxly religious in poems, the description can be painfully true.

Among the most competent of these, the religious motive can, at times, result in a wise and independent fusion of older traditions (the medieval, the Ignatian, the Metaphysical, the Puritan) with the dictates of the American cultural landscape (the culture made landscape is one of our dominant metaphors). One thinks of the younger Robert Lowell, of the metaphysically ecstatic moments in a poetry like that of Theodore Roethke, of the late, troubled, "wisdom" poetry of John Berryman. But for those with a balanced concern for both the religious and the poetic word, there is always a cost. The cost is frequently one (especially in the recent currents of taste) of critical attention, and without critical attention is, of course, reputation. Such has been the case, it seems, with Vassar Miller.

When Miller's work first began to appear (*Adam's Footprint*, 1956), the mood was Eliotesque, more favorable to the religious poet; by 1983, when her most recent book (*Struggling to Swim on Concrete*) appeared, it definitely was not. Even the titles themselves seem to suggest a movement from Edenic promise to cruel struggle. In the interim, despite the attention of major poet-commentators such as James Wright, Denise Lever-tov, and Howard Nemerov (mostly early-on) and an abundance of anthology appearances and reviews of the intervening five volumes, almost no in-depth criticism or biography has appeared. This is true despite her sub-stantial growth and adaptation to change in style over the period. One aspect of her work remained consistent-ly the same: she remained an orthodox, Christian re-ligious poet, though not one dependent, except casually, on theology as subject matter. She is also rarely Biblical.

It is true, however, that her opposition to the modern sense of self in poetry may sometimes present a work which stands somewhere between poetry and prayer, a poem so ''self-consuming'' (in the sense which has recently been applied to George Herbert) (3) that it is nearly unliterary in its seeming directness; bare, image-less. Such a poem is one to which she gave special positional emphasis in her second book(*Wage War on Silence*, 1960), by drawing that book's title from it. The concepts of ceremony and silence which are elemental to this poem return in a much later poem, too so that they seem of emphatic importance. The poem involved here is titled ''Without Ceremony'':

> Except ourselves, we have no other prayer;
> Our needs are sores upon our nakedness.
> We do not have to name them; we are here.
> And You who made the eye can see no less.
> We fall, not on our knees, but on our hearts,
> A posture humbler far and more downcast;
> While Father Pain instructs us in the arts
> Of praying, hunger is the worthiest fast.
> We find ourselves where tongues cannot wage war
> On silence (farther mystics never flew)
> But on the common wings of what we are,
> Borne on the wings of what we bear toward You,

O Word in whom our wordiness dissolves,
When we have not a prayer except ourselves.
(*SNP*, p. 123)
But the barren tone of this poem is designed, sincere
and artful. True, without careful attention to the design
and art, one might categorize the poem as simply born
from that kind of Calvinist-oriented hatred of ego before
God that could make the sensitive Puritan self a living
hell, sometimes one veritably suicidal. And it seems
true, too, that the Puritan is one main line of religious
culture (not theology) on which this poet draws. The
characterization of "Father Pain," who is the instructor
in prayer seems consistent with that assumption, and
mediation through Christ is abstracted to the purely
theological (or "mystical"?) level of the Word, here not
"made flesh" except as the unrecognized, or unformed,
mute "wordiness," which the Word absorbs.

But it must be seen that whatever sincerity and
sympathy condition the irony of this expression from a
poet, the personless persona voice of "we" strengthens
it. It is the institutional voice of the group which
emanates not from a sense of communion (we are here
"without ceremony"), but from the common human
tragedy of separation, isolation, aloneness. The ironically
controlling sense begins and ends the poem: "When we
have not a prayer except ourselves."

Because of what might be called the dramatic irony
of its method, "Without Ceremony" is reduced from the
complexity of expression of the tradition from which it
may derive: the meditative metaphysicality of George
Herbert or John Donne, or the "Terrible Sonnets" of
Father Gerard Hopkins; it is nearer in its verbal style to
the Puritan plain song than to the metaphysical har-
mony-in-discord. But the "music" here is atonal, modern, mimetic of its culture.

In Howard Nemerov's *Poets on Poetry*, Miller called
"Without Ceremony" an "awkward poem," because

"waging war on silence is an awkward thing to do."
The volume title *Wage War on Silence*, suggests, she
said, "the very nature of poetry, which is war waged
with the silence of misunderstanding between men, with
the silence of God that Christ endured on the cross,
summing up in himself our individual endurances." (5)
It is the poetic crying out against the silence, then,
which imitates the crying out of Jesus from the Cross,
and it is poetic "ceremony," which gives expression.
In "Without Ceremony," believers are left as the isolated crowd, the "we" who "have not a prayer except
ourselves." In a passage from a much later poem ("Approaching Nada," 1977) Miller suggests the required
connection: "Somewhere between silence and ceremony
springs the Word,/the wellhead of all hush feeding the
roots/of tongues. . . .Listen, whoever/tunes an ear."
(*SNP*, p. 123)

It is straining this metaphor of the Spirit too far to
suggest that it requires, beyond the linkage of the
institutional congregation and the poet, the linkage of
the religious American poet and the literary audience?
The "awkward" quality of the poem is, then, engen-
dered in the pain of its struggle. It is easy enough to
understand how, among the pious well-wishers of christian capital investment whose heavenly bond-shares must
always go up, such poetic pain, if considered at all,
must be "awkward." Harder to understand is the contemporary indifference to this kind of poetic genuiness
among those who, whether believing or not, ought to
respect its artistic value and struggle and, in context, its
marked success.

Part of our difficulty in accepting a poem like "Without Ceremony," in order to understand it, today, stems,
no doubt, from our history-long reaction-formation a-
gainst Puritanism in literary terms, by which we fail to
recognize the potentials of that brave "errand into the
wilderness" which Puritanism, however harshly, contrib-

uted. That this failure of recognition is not Vassar Miller's is evident in a poem published in the volume immediately following *Wage War on Silence*, entitled "Note to the Reader," in which she notes that: "This book, these sheets of paper you pick up/and toss aside for being only ink--/this is soul's sweat and bile, black slag, outcrop/of heart's New England, apples of its stone." (7) No writer could have expressed an aspect of the religious poet's pain more forcefully, and the lines seem to me to express, too, the soured idealism of our social history, its scarred and blood-soaked frontier success, expressed as poetic experience in the shadow of this Christian poet's sense of Fall and Crucifixion. A poem from the 1976 collection, *Small Change*, expresses this in calling Jesus a "pioneer in pain" (in "Accepting"): "Lord, serene on your symbol/you plant your flag/on pain's last outpost. . . .Against your side woe's wildness/strings its red vine/and shadows your face./ Then name this bloody ground/firm underfoot/home, however homely." (8)

The strongest poems in her work, indeed, seem to be those expressing the separation, isolation, aloneness of metaphoric or cultural landscape. A poem of this kind which brings the elements of my title into closer connection is "Loneliness." In it the paradoxical crying out against the silence and the half-loving yielding to it element the "aloneness":

> So deep is this silence
> that the insects, the birds,
> the talk of the neighbors in the distance,
> the whir of the traffic, the music
> are its only voices
> and do not contradict it.
>
> So deep is this crying
> that the silence, the hush,

the quiet, the stillness, the not speaking,
the never hearing a word
are only the surge
of its innumerable waters.

This silence, this crying
O my God, is my country
with Yours the sole footstep besides my own.
Save me amid its landscapes
so terrible, strange
I am almost in love with them! (9)

Here it seems that the search for poetic self-defin-
ition involves the traditionally meditative companionship
with God (called on almost profanely in regard to the
poet's country) as a witness to a kind of cautious
treading in enemy territory (with God, on the poetic
"war" path?) This is the "almost loved" country of
silence (that silence) itself a mysterious native tongue
requiring translation). It is the country both native and
terrible, a wilderness of poetic identity into which she
walks with the single, silent "presence" to use De
Tocqueville's term differently, of the protecting Guide.
This is the country of aloneness longing for completion,
and, naturally enough, its final terms are those, however
fearful, of love: the poet's for the audience, one believes, as well as for the land and the Lord.

To be straightforward with the reader about Miller's
sense of the lacking critical audience in this "longing,"
she did not assert it as a conscious problem, although
she recognized religious "difference" as being one
which could bring rejection:

His fellow poets didn't exactly like it
when Eliot got religion and viewed his
conversion as detrimental to his poetry. If
he had ever recanted, the good Christian

bretheren who regard him as a trophy for
the Lord would not have liked it any
better. Enough said. All of us would enjoy
being at ease in Zion, and, if we are not,
we cry "woe!" (10)

But for all this cheerful objectivity, she could not
help but suffer from those conflicts which I have tried to
clarify. If her physical sufferings were, obviously, the
basis of much of her expression of loneliness and pain,
her sense of the culturally self-consuming (self-sacri-
ficing?) elements in her art, identified with the Crucified, obviously, too, gave her moral pain. The late, long
poem "Approaching Nada" (she identified the word as
meaning "ineffable," indicating the approach to poet-
cally expressed mystery) she sees poetry as a part of
the landscape of crucifixion: "These poets of the Nada/
obeyed Him. As poets, mystics of/the bruising thing/
climb up bloody concretes/to leave nailed high/white
pieces of themselves." (11)
And the cruelty of the "concretes" of the poetic
mystic's earth are localized in the American scene near
Phoenix, Arizona ("Phoenix" becomes, too, the poet's
later name for the Christ-identification) in "Approaching
Nada":

Here where all rivers run sand,
this taking-off pad to deep space,
the air too thin for my lungs,
the water too scant for my mouth,
the gold light too rich for my flesh,
hungry for flabbier fare
than even the loaf and the wine
served sparsely on every Lord's Day
hungry for dust on my dust
slightly more damp than the tomb's.
My Lord and my Christ, dare I come

here where the sun shrieks Thy name,
here where the wind rasps hosannas
in atonal chords on my ears,
asking the giftings of grace
sealed with these fire-signs of death! (12)

American and individual as this scene is, it also
echoes the wasteland imagery of much modern religious
poetry. Consider Rilke's Mary, soliloquizing in "Before
the Passion":

O if you wanted this you should not have been
allowed to spring forth through a woman's body:
saviors should be quarried in the mountains,
whence the hard is broken from the hard.
Are you yourself not sorry so to lay waste
your beloved valley? See my weakness:
I have nothing but brooks of milk and tears,
And you were always in excess. (13)

Yet even in so brief a passage, there seems a
difference in concept as well as approach: Rilke's Virgin
Mary is an accepted religious symbol (or, if the reader
wishes, an accepted religious "myth") in his literary
culture, the humanizing of Mary as woman, thereby,
becomes the poet's responsibility. Jesus is a distant (one
must say Crucial) figure of the "Nada" the inexpressible final "Word" in Miller, the human figure of Jesus
seeming to have no human immediacy available to the
poet, only the prophetic signs of Him in silence, root
and Word. The third section of "Approaching Nada"
returns to the terms of "Without Ceremony" again with
no lesser pain, only a reduced irony, a more direct
expression of the poet's understanding of role: "Somewhere between silence and ceremony springs the Word,/
the wellhead of all hush feeding the roots/of tongues
whether of men or angels, interchange/between us and

your world./Listen, whoever tunes an ear.'' (14)

The difference seems partially between Miller's Protestant (intellectualizing) and Rilke's Catholic (visual-
izing, symbolizing) poetic culture, perhaps. But the difference is also in American culture's rejection (yes, even
for its Catholics) of all spiritual history except its own.
Writing on Vassar Miller's *Struggling to Swim on Concrete*, D.E. Richardson most wisely, I think, observes:

> The tradition that we should have no
> tradition but a landscape and a sky and
> our own aloneness with God is of course
> new and old American. . .tradition; its or-
> igins may be traced even beyond Ameri-
> can shores--as the very name of Words-
> worth will testify. That we live in a land-
> scape without history is a characteristic
> American attitude; it forces us to deny the
> truth that the landscape itself has his-
> tory. . . .

And, one might add, that we have a history in it,
and that the landscape itself is dependent upon the
history that we unite with its own. Richardson goes on
to comment on the "compromise" this unyielding myth-
os of historical timelessness requires when it confronts a
revealed version of "history" in religion. (15) Beyond
the quite understandable necessity of avoiding Bible-
thumping mindlessness or ritualistic dogmatism this
"compromise" may be one way of expressing the unwil-
lingness of the Christian believers among our poets to
express any religous committment openly, as Vassar
Miller has. One thinks of the late John Berryman in his
fierce defense against being accused of being anything
but free-thinking in his poetry, even as he attempted to
return that poetry to a connection with a renewed (if
very troubled) Catholicism. He was, on balance, ap-

parently, a Catholic agnostic attending mass "every Sunday," but unbelieving in the divinity of Christ. He told the interviewer Peter Stitt of the poems of "piety" he had been writing, and commented on the likely hostility of the literary public to these (published posthumously in *Delusions, etc.*, 1970):

> Some of the poems are threatening. . .just as some people find me threatening. . . just as some people find me threatening-- to be in a room with me drives them crazy. . .And there is a grave piety in the last poems, which is going to trouble a lot of people. You know the country is full of atheists and they really are going to find themselves threatened by these poems. . . Then there are others who detest them-- they don't call them insincere, but they just can't believe it. (15)

Some years ago, I wondered in an article on Berryman whether his seeming desperation at this stage was not the psychological fear of the annihilating element in the identification with Christ, his fear of acting out his own, in the shadow of his father's self-slaughter. (16) If so, one can only wonder what forces, historical, cultural, or otherwise can so cruelly and unnaturally pervert what has been the schemata of good men and women and great artists in other times and places over thousands of years.

To put it less emotively, however inevitable (and, yes, even Constitutionally necessary) the separation of church and poetic statement may have been for us, one cannot believe that it has been good for the mind and soul of American Christianity to have its expressions of Faith reduced to bourgeois smugness, for American literature to have seen some of its best talents driven into alien relation to it, for American political democracy to have been deprived of the moral zeal of any but the most embarrassing, or threatening of its political proponents of "Christian" ideology.

That Vassar Miller, bravely, did not add to all our failures in this regard is greatly to her credit. The tough consistency of this woman's character merits, and the artistic merit of her art deserves better attention than it has had.

Vassar Miller and Her Peers: A Causerie

THOMAS WHITBREAD

As Wallace Stevens accurately asserts, in one of his *Adagia*, "in poetry, you must love the words, the ideas and the images and rhythms with all your capacity to love anything at all." (1) False poets are embarrassed by the fervor of Stevens' remark. All true poets will give assent to it as splendid aesthetic theory; but it is a rare and great true poet who can put the theory into practice. To do so requires talent, hard work, and above all a tenacious dedication to the rich possibilities of language--of the words, ideas, images, rhythms--as the chief love of one's life. One such rare poet is Vassar Miller. In her poetry we sense an implicit devotion to Stevens' emotional imperative, a creative enactment of its "you must love the words" that is extraordinarily intense, pervasive, and profound.

Vassar Miller's deep and inherent love of words is intensified by her often expressed need for them as weapons in her war on silence. The word "silence" appears many times in her work, often as the enemy--as in "His mind, bright bird, forever trapped in silence" ("Spastic Child"). At times, when she is questing towards "the Word," she may question whether words, words, words aren't a buzzing hindrance to the possibility of attaining mystical vision; at such times, "silence," sometimes capitalized, may take on positive connotations. But she uses words to say so. And in one of her greatest poems, "Approaching Nada," it is a complex word-- "Phoenix"--which gloriously expresses her sense of the Grail. Most of the time, Miller is more self-aware skeptic than would-be mystic; more like Auden than like Eliot. Like so many of the earlier word-lovers whose poems she knows and loves, Miller is an ardent laborer in this imperfect world, seeking through poetry to "Make a vineyard of the curse." (2)

To read, reread, and reread again, in chronological order, the *Selected and New Poems, 1950-1980*, is to see and hear a poet sure-footed in versification from the start, who becomes surer-footed as she goes along. Like Theodore Roethke, Robert Lowell, W.S. Merwin, and Adrienne Rich, Miller begins by writing in various strict or "closed" forms, using rhyme schemes. Like Roethke and Lowell, but unlike Merwin and Rich, she continues occasionally to use strict forms even after, in early mid-career, she becomes more free or "open" in versification, experiments diversely, and fully finds her own "voice," or voices. While noticing these formal developments, I shall single out several of the earlier poets to whom Vassar seems closest, whether by verbal echo, allusion, or affinity.

The first poem in the standard edition of John Keats is his "Imitation of Spenser." In *Selected and New Poems*, Miller has no "Imitation of Hopkins," but several of the poems reprinted from her first volume, *Adam's Footprint* (1956), show a delight in heavy alliteration within strong pentameters, and the sonnet, "The Final Hunger" (*SNP*, p. 16), sounds and looks like a mesh of Gerard Manley Hopkins' "The Windhover" with one of his "terrible sonnets" in the way it begins:

> Hurl down the nerve-gnarled body hurtling head-
> Long into sworls of shade-hush. Plummeting, keep
> The latch of eyelids shut so outleap
> Care's claws.
>
> (*SNP*, p. 16)

Recall the way "The Windhover" opens:

> I caught this morning morning's minion, king-

> dom of daylight's dauphin, dapple-dawn-drawn
>   / Falcon . . . (3)

Near the end of "The Final Hunger" there is an embedded parenthetical exclamation, reminiscent of the famous "(my God!)" near the end of Hopkins' "Carrion Comfort":

> Sun-sword night-sheathed, lie never between
>   / (have pity!)
> Between me and my love, between me and
>   / the vaulting
> Down the dense sweetness of oblivion.
>
>   (*SNP*, p. 16)

The last line, though, is not Hopkinsian; it sounds more like the rhetorically elevated, somewhat melodramatic way in which Enda St. Vincent Millay (an often fine poet unjustly ignored in today's groves of academe) ends some of the sonnets in her 52-poem sequence, *Fatal Interview*. For instance:

> The wind of their endurance, driving south,
> Flattened your words against your speaking
>   / mouth. (4)

The connections between Miller and Millay are in terms of bravura performance and the sense of an ending that is unquestionably and thumpingly final. Also, "dense sweetess of oblivion" verbally echoes the last sonnet of *Fatal Interview*, where in "Mortal Endymion" is said to have "poured/The hot and sorrowful sweetness of the dust" into the "crystal body" of the Moon-goddess, who as a result now "wanders mad," and of whose "altered state" Endymion is ordered to "Oblivious Lie!" (5) Millay, to be just, is seldom so wrought up; at her best she can often be powerfully straightforward, as

is Miller in the superb eighth line of "The Final
Hunger": "Sleep, the sole lover that I take to bed."
Elinor Wylie's "Wild Peaches," IV (which begins,
"Down to the Puritan marrow of my bones/There's
something in this richness I hate," (6) lurks strongly
behind Miller's poem in for austere quatrains, "Puritan
Delight." And the line, "The muted tragedies of moth
and mote," (*SNP*, p. 14) from "Spastic Child," could
have been penned in fading ink by Thomas Hardy. But
the most influential master figuring in the poems from
Adam's Fooprint is Edwin Arlington Robinson. This is
not surprising, since Miller's M.A. thesis (University of
Houston, 1950) was on mysticism in Robinson's poetry.
Her homage to Robinson has several aspects. "Columbus Dying," in versification expertise and melancholy
mood, resembles one of Robinson's more somber Tilbury
Town poems, in which a seeker misses connections with
the divine--Columbus "found a world and put to scorn
his scorners," but "missed the angels guarding the four
corners" (7)--and comes to a disillusioned, sad end, as
did Miller's Columbus, with a "vision of men" as

> Gum-footed flies glued to a spinning ball.
> Whether they tumble off earth's edge or crawl
> Till dropped dead in their tracks from vertigo,
> He deemed would make no difference at all.
>
> (*SNP*, p. 17)

The poem is in two six-line stanzas, each stanza sport-
ing an *abaaba* rhyme scheme; "scorners" and "corners"
constitute the *b*-rhyme in stanza one. I call attention to
this feature because the deft deployment of feminine
rhymes for variation and special effect is an important
technical ability which Miller learned early from Robinson and has continued to use at times throughout her
career.

"Revival" shows this ability in spades. The poem is

in six pentameter quatrains. The end-rhymes in stanza one are entirely feminine; in stanza five, entirely masculine. In stanzas two and three, the a-rhymes are masculine, the b-rhymes feminine. In stanzas four and six, the a-rhymes are feminine, the b-rhymes masculine. For a while, the rhyming virtuosity adds to the playfulness and wit with which the poem starts, as a humorous satire of a fire-breathing preacher ("Good Brother Botts through gesture and gyration/Of fervor flung himself") and his haughtily smug flock ("How grace had cushioned every pious rump"). When in mid-career the poem turns solemn, focusing on "a solitary woman" ("Her face, a hurricane of meekness frozen"), the rhymes cease to be witty, and Miller achieves a simile, like many of Robinson's of the most touching simplicity:

Botts wheedled her with Heaven's gaudy gold,
But she'd watched folks limp deathward
            /doubt by doubt
And when he howled of Hell, she felt as cold
As Kitchen stoves are when their fires go out.

In the last stanza, an ironically unnoticed miracle occurs, and Miller's language resembles Robinson's at his most exalted:

Yet while we gawked and Brother Botts decried her,
When One named Truth men tried in Pilate's hall
Rose up, a rapier of flame, beside her,
Nobody saw--and she saw least of all.   (*SNP*, p. 20)

The mastery of rhyming in this poem reminds me of that Robinson achieves in his great "Eros Turannos."
    "Mirror for a Lady" is very good, almost as good a poem in praise of a live woman as is Robinson's "For a Dead Lady," which it at times resembles in diction, imagery, and alliteration (Miller writes, "We, too, be-

long within her halls/Wherein the fustian of our ways/
Shimmers to satins of her poise;" Robinson speaks of
"The flowing wonder of her ways,/Whereof no language
may requite/The shifting and the many-shaded"). (8)
Both ladies have "grace." But Miller's live lady has
also "wrought an ease of elegance/And made a home of
ceremony," (*SNP*, p. 21) achieving what W.B. Yeats
wishes in "A Prayer for my Daughter" and what
Richard Wilbur celebrates in his "Ceremony."

"Adam's Footprint," like "Open House," the first
poem in Roethke's first volume, is in three six-line
stanzas; but its resonances are more with Andrew Mar-
vell (of "The Garden") and, again, Robinson. But of all
these early poems, my favorite is "Revival." In it Miller
has absorbed all the lessons she has learned from
Robinson, while at the same time achieving an ease of
diction and that sure control of her voice which is
characteristic of her mature poetry, in which she is
effectively humorous, solemn, or ironic--and, for that
matter, elevated or plain--when and as she wills. Fur-
thermore, it is as if the mastery of strict formal elements achieved in "Revival" liberates Miller into the
freer and more experimental poems that dominate her
work from now on. She knows she can write a fine
poem in a strict form whenever she wants too--and she
occasionally does so.

Near the end of his brief life, Keats wrote a friend
that he was trying to become less like Milton, more like
Shakespeare. Something similar may be said about Miller: she rapidly becomes less like Robinson or Hopkins,
more her own powerful and varied self. W.H. Auden's
example may have helped her develop a flowing ease in
rhyme while adopting a public persona as a communal
spokesperson, audible in "Love Song for the Future,"
which opens,

To our ruined vineyards come,
Little foxes, for your share
Of our blighted grapes, the tomb
Readied for our common lair.
Ants, we open you the cupboard;
Flee no more the heavy hand
Harmless as a vacant scabbard
Since our homes like yours are sand.

(*SNP*, p. 26)

A formally Shakespearean sonnet, "Paradox," reminds
Denise Levertov of George Herbert; it reminds me of
John Donne, especially in its ending:

Blind me to blindness, deafen me to deafness.
So will Your gifts of sight and hearing plunder
My eyes with lightning and my ears with thunder.

(*SNP*, p. 32)

This resonates with Donne's *Holy Sonnet 14*: ". . .for
I,/Except You entrall me, never shall be free,/Nor ever
chaste, except You ravish me." (8) But the close of
"'Though He Slay Me'" is completely heartsblood Vassar Miller:

I lulled to a like darkness with Your no,
No, no, still no, the echo of Your yes
Distorted among the crevices and caves
Of the coiled ear which deep in its abyss
Resolves to music all Your negatives.

(*SNP*, p. 33)

"Music" here is a metaphor for right speech as sovereign antidote for all pain; and Miller's words enact
that speech. In some moods, in fact, for Miller speech
equals life:

I am sorry to sing you
no more melodious song, yet only
the taste of its notes biting my tongue remind me,
sometimes, that I am alive.

(*SNP*, p. 39)

The above quatrain concludes "Bread-and-Butter Letter Not Sent," the first poem from *My Bones Being
Wiser* (1963). Notice in this quatrain the absence of
rhyme, the variety of line lengths, the abandonment of
the convention of capitals at the start of each line.
Many, if not most, of the rest of the poems in the
volume at hand--pages 34-157, to be precise--are in this
more low-key, conversational, the-impact-of-every-word-
counts mode. Denise Levertov, in her Preface, puts this
every-word-counts achievement very nicely: "These are
poems that seem to call for something other than print
and paper--one imagines them carved in stone, engraved
in metal." As Levertov says, "the incised words go
deep." (9) And, from now on, obvious influences are
few and far between; verbal echoes are replaced by
deliberate allusions (for instance, the stark use of Marianne Moore, "For I am the toad/in my imagined
garden," in "*Raison D'Etre*") and, more importantly,
felt affinities between herself and certain poetic equals.
Most of Miller's poems employ the "I," and speak
forth essences or aspects of her state of being. Some of
the earlier poems are "For" or "To" particular people--
"N.C.," "B.M.E.," "Katherine"--and the superbly runic
and incantatory "For a Christening" is "For my first
nephew." Aside from the "Lady" of elegance and
ceremony, and the wonderful "Good Brother Botts," the
chief characters other than the "I" in these poems, and
in many later poems as well, are God and Christ. What
about other human beings? Reading the poems in sequence, I was delighted to find "Belated Lullaby," with
its praise of "Bach's ordered ecstasy." Soon after I was

stuck by two brilliant dramatic monologues. One, "Judas," is in the form of a Petrarchan sonnet; it ends,

> Praise Peter, who could weep
> His sin away, but never see me where
> I hang, huge teardrop on the cheek of night.
>
> (*SNP*, p. 57)

The other, "Pontius Pilate Discusses the Proceedings of the Last Judgment" begins, "Unfortunate. Yet how was I to know," and concludes,

> Our gambles looked the same. We lost.
> *He* really and truly was the Son of God?
> I'm not surprised. The gods will play some joke--
> And then get angry every time it works!
>
> (*SNP*, p. 75)

Shades of Robert Browning! But the tone, idioms, and daringly extended sequence of six run-over lines earlier in this blank verse masterpiece are *echt* Miller. Further evidence of subject matter beyond the self occurs in Miller's vivid celebration of Sophie Tucker, "Dirge in Jazz Time" (*SNP*, p. 78), which is also one of her mature poems showing absolute mastery of strict form.

Though it is hard to prove, I think not only Browning but Auden and T.S. Eliot may have helped show the way to Miller for her own highly original dramatic monologues and poems in public voice or on public subjects. I sense a definite affinity with Eliot when Miller is being sarcastic about demonstrative religious gymnastics, or the hoop-là of humility--"a whining importunity/wherein you grimace and gesture/and writhe and gyrate/and wriggle and jump/in the postures of peace" (*SNP*, p. 55)--or mordant about what to do to show charity and attain glory:

The dust I kick up irritates the nose.
What shall I do then? Shun strong drink
                    / as you did?
Read Scripture every night? Keep Sunday strictly?
Or practice with a different set of gimmicks?
Eat fish on Friday? Go to Mass each morning?
Or else fall into trances? Speak in tongues?
Rembering you, I think not.

                                        (*SNP*, p. 70)

The affinity of these lines (from the fine "Remembering Aunt Helen") that I sense with Eliot is with the mordantly sarcastic passage in "The Dry Salvages," V, from "To communicate with Mars, converse with spirits," through "To explore the womb, or tomb, or dreams; all these are usual/Pastimes and drugs, and features of the press. . ."(10) But Eliot's tone is more world-weary than Miller's; her words are a bit more biting, more ferocious, more electric.

In none of Miller's publicly oriented poems is she more powerfully ferocious and controlled than in "Culture Shock" set off by man's walking on the moon, and "Age of Aquarius, Age of Assassins," wherein the shooting of George Wallace inspires her to address him in one of the great poems of this century:

Conniver, my nonkissing cousin, bastard,
                    / my brother,
this poet bereft of heroes and slightly below
the angels, and therefore Satan's small sister
                    / salutes you
to question, Which land shall I leave now and
                    / head for what other?
From people committing such crimes where
                    / should I go
without sloughing the human skin in whose
                    / guise a crank shoots you?

When A-bombs, H-bombs, the whole alphabet
/ of our guilt
indicts me no more than the ovens roasting
/ the Jews,
no more than my cronies' mutual murder
/ by inches?
You, more petty than yesterday's paper, what
/ have we built
since one week, two weeks ago, since Adam
/ was news,
but the House of the Shoe Fitting Best the
/ Harder it Pinches!

Not that I with precision tools could construct
/ the house better
than you, driving wooden pegs with your
/ stone-headed hatchet.
For man is a chronic case regressing, improving,
regressing, twisting in bed to find a cool spot,
/ turned bitter
when he finds the sheet burning again where
/ his bones touch it.
Yet, there's some hope (though, by God,
/ none by you)
because he keeps moving.

(*SNP*, p. 99)

The white-hot intensity of every burning word in this
poem is enhanced by the strict form; it is as if each
packed line nearly bursts off the page into outrage, its
rip tide rigorously held in check by the brilliant rhyme
scheme. What mastery! I suspect Robert Penn Warren
would give his eyeteeth to have written this poem.

Another of Miller's greatest poems is the five-part
"Approaching Nada," written in Phoenix, Arizona,
March 7-10, 1977. The intense circumstances of its
composition, and the quality of the poetic results, are

reminiscent of Rilke's almost entranced creation of the
Sonnets to Orpheus and the *Duino Elegies*. It may be
that the distance from Houston, the sudden entrance
into a desert landscape of starkness and beauty instantly
and instinctually felt as an expansion of her self, and
who knows what else of mystery and grace, combined to
liberate Miller into a brilliant mosaic, wherein Quaker,
Aztec, and Catholic come together. Hamlet might have
found, as she does, Christ the Phoenix, Abbe Bremond,
Juan de la Cruce, and Teresa de Avila are "poets of
the Nada," "poets, mystics of/the bruising thing," and,
a real breakthrough, Miller can write freely about her
family. Earlier, she remembered her Aunt Helen mov
ingly, and one poem had brief, veiled references to her
"dead mother" and her "father." Now, in "Approaching Nada," she writes vividly, openly, anecdotally of her
great-grandfather, her grandmother, her father's father,
and "Gentler Vannah, sister/to my own mother." This
fertile breakthrough into familial subject matter yields
immediate further fruit in "Subterfuge," a loving memory of her father; in the tenderly compassionate and
forgiving "Lullaby For My Mother"; and in that lullaby's somber counterpart, the therapeutically purgative
"Dark Mother":

> My mother, you, when well, forgot me,
> / your first-born
> you never bore, whom no man got upon you
> / save a dream
> more childish than your youngest: you
> / desired a doll,
> cunning, if broken. But when it moved
> and howled and kicked and spat, you threw
> / it down
> with disappointment and disgust. It's too late.
> I'm nearly as old as you are. Nobody can
> mother us, either one, save that black mother,

kindly, if cruel, whose arms reach for us all
drawing us down and down and back and back
into her winding sheets of womb. Nobody
            / likes her summons
late in the evening. She sings her lullaby
through a mouth cracking and cackling from
            / long calling.

                                        (*SNP*, p. 133)

In this honest, strong, but not bitter poem--so unlike
Sylvia Plath's "Daddy"--Miller moves from her own
actual mother to "that black mother," Mother Earth as
Death, in diction, imagery, and alliteration not unlike
those Wallace Stevens uses about a similar "mother" at
the end of his late poem, "Madame La Fleurie":

The black fugatos are strumming the
            / blacknesses of black. . .
The thick strings stutter the final gutterals.
He does not lie there remembering the blue-jay
            / jay, say the jay.
His grief is that his mother should feed on him,
            / himself and what he saw,
In that distant chamber, a bearded queen,
            / wicked in her dead light. (11)

This resonance between Miller and Stevens is a sport
in its particularity. Much more pervasive is an affinity
between these two absolute lovers of words, an affinity
which manifests itself in a certain kind of poem each
often writes: a muted, meditative, subduedly intense
kind of poem, in three to seven tercets, with unrhymed
lines of varying lengths. Miller's such poems include
"Aubade," "Love's Eschatology," "A Bird in the
Hand," "Bitterness," "Addict," "Slump," "Cycle,"
"Encounter," "Accepting," and "Listening to Rain at
Night." Among Stevens' are "The Snow Man," "An-

other Weeping Woman,'' "The Death of a Soldier,''
"The Brave Man," "Poetry Is a Destructive Force,"
"World Without Peculiarity,'' "Lebensweisheitspielerei,''
"The Planet on the Table," "Not Ideas About the Thing
But the Thing Itself,'' and "Of Mere Being." I urge the
reader to read all these poems and sense their kinspirit-
edness of mood, diction, rhythm. For one example, take
Miller's "Cycle":

> My body, weary traveler,
> in an oasis drinks
> from pools of sleep.
>
> Its cells, all its million tongues,
> lap up the dark coolness.
> Love never went
>
> more naked to bed than when
> my body shrugs off
> logic's gold sheath
>
> in the black irrational,
> water which one day
> will drink my body.
>   (*SNP*, p. 88)

Then savor Stevens' "Lebensweisheitspielerei," which
ends,

> Little by little, the poverty
> Of autumnal space becomes
> A look, a few words spoken.
>
> Each person completely touches us
> With what he is and as he is,
> In the stale grandeur of annihilation. (12)

The two poets are unique yet similar: non-identical twins of imagination, peers of the populace of the heart.

Roethke, in "A Rouse for Stevens," called Stevens "imagination's prince." The term applies equally well to Richard Wilbur, who once told me of what he amusedly called a kind of "laying on of hands": at a meeting of the Poetry Society of America in 1951, at which the ruddy and portly Stevens received an award and ordered double martinis all round, Stevens clapped Wilbur on the shoulder and said, "You have the right stuff." Wilbur has championed Miller's poetry for more than three decades. And it was Wilbur who in 1961, while in Houston as a Ford-sponsored adjunct to the Alley Theater, first told me to read and revel in Miller's verses. It seems meet, therefore, that I end this causerie with a poem of Wilbur. In "Cottage Street, 1953," he evokes a very strained tea party, hostessed by his mother-in-law, Edna Ward; the guests are 21-year-old Sylvia Plath and her worried mother, Wilbur and his wife. As he says, recreating the occasion,

> It is my office to exemplify
> The published poet in his happiness,
> Thus cheering Sylvia, who has wished to die. . .

But nothing can cheer Sylvia. The party and the day run down. The lives go on, though two will end in very different ways:

> And Edna Ward shall die in fifteen years,
> After her eight-and-eighty summers of
> Such grace and courage as permit no tears
> The thin hand reaching out, the last word *love*,
>
> Outliving Sylvia who, condemned to live,
> Shall study for a decade, as she must,
> To state at last her brilliant negative

In poems free and helpless and unjust. (13)

My point is that Vassar Miller is *not* like Sylvia Plath: Miller's poems are never "helpless," never "unjust." She is like Edna Ward. In the teeth of all the pain and suffering of her human lot, she has gracefully and courageously spun words into diversely shaped, beautiful, and moving poems. Her conscious craft and artistry in learning from, absorbing, and allowing herself in her independence to at times rotate in electromagnetic affinity with other planetary poets provide a model for emulation. In her total love of words, the ideas and the images and rhythms with all her capacity to love anything at all, she has enriched our lives.

Blood in the Bone:
Vassar Miller's Prosody

BRUCE KELLNER

For longer than the thirty years or so that Vassar Miller has been publishing her poems, rhyme has struck all too many solid citizens as well as parasites in the landscape of *vers libre* with suspicion. As if they were familiar with the origins of the word from Latin's *rhythmos* and Greek's *rhuthmos*, they have found rhythm equally unworthy, except as their own breathing may on occasion have measured it. The quainter time poems used to keep might be suitable for anthologies, but out of insolence or incompetence most poets and poetasters choose to ignore it. Lamentably, what substitutions they offer prosody's catalog are rarely strong enough to perform a new trick of the trade. There are exceptions, of course, a number of poets whose organic forms grow so inextricably from their content that the two not only are inseparable but the one--either one, form or content--does not survive without the other. Vassar Miller is that even rarer exception, a poet at ease with tradition in temples others have erected and in nomad's tents she herself can raise. The spectacular sequence that concludes *Struggling to Swim on Concrete*, "Love's Bitten Tongue," is a fair example of her comfort in territory where squatters' rights have left little space to spread: twenty-two English sonnets locked together through each concluding line's serving as a subsequent first line, in every instance altered punctuation or syntax extending the sequence or illuminating what has gone before. The unassailable integrity of "Defense Rests" gasping its syllables in uneven lines to speak faith's desperation; or the breathless despair of the single-sentenced "On Approaching My Birthday," both a grammatical unit and a

life's sentence on her; or the unpunctuated free associ-
ations in "Whitewash of Houston," condemning the
present's vulgarity, mourning the past's innocence, are
only three of many of her own especial scaffoldings
owing no allegiance to tradition. Temple or tent, the
prosody is always her own.

The fact that so often Vassar Miller has operated
within the confines of established prosodic patterns may
persuade readers that she is somehow engaged in a
craft. More likely she is crafty, with the subtle duplicity
that word implies. Elsewhere in this collection of Vassar
Miller's work, readers have addressed themselves to her
content, and many of them have paid more than passing
acknowledgment to the forms it has taken; but I would
reverse that order here and stare down the mechanism.
Surely no one reads the poems unmoved or untouched
by their staggering images, the extravagance of their
metaphors, their honed phrases, and it is right that our
attention be so directed. The process of making or
building a poem never mandates scrutiny; sometimes
readers remark the balance and the closure, impressed
with the oddity of an unnameable perfection, but more
often their concern is with what happens in a poem
rather than how it happens. Thomas Kinsella--another
poet attentive to form--asks in an early piece "if the
simple primrose show[s]/That mighty work went on
below/Before it grew. . ." (1). I have wrenched that
observation out of context, but it illustrates a point
which, sufficiently examined, will prove out any poem's
triumph or defeat. I dare say Marianne Moore was
referring to content when she demanded poems be
"imaginary gardens with real toads in them" (2), but it
is equally true that those "imaginary gardens" do not
bloom without the ugly tangle of roots and runners deep
in dirt, the compost of other seasons' leavings, the
chicken dung or sheep shit or whatever the gardener
dug in and dug into for sustenance, the underground

labor to let light break in new growth.

I have no idea whether Vassar Miller is familiar with W.H. Auden's observation that the "poet's problem in the twentieth century is not how to write iambics but how not to write in them from automatic habit when they are not to our genuine purpose" (3), nor his reference to the tidy household resulting when the master is good to his servants, Rhyme and Meter, nor indeed his sorrow for some Robinson Crusoe, laboring on poetry's isle, doing his own cooking and washing up, with some resultant "squalor" more often than some "original and impressive" free verse (4). Vassar Miller made herself clear on similar subjects, however, in her interview with Karla M. Hammond: "A good free verse poem weaves its form out of itself, but much of what passes for poetry today reads like a grocery list or a postcard, as if the poet slapped down the first words that came to mind without benefit of passion or precision" (5). She acknowledge that "too much artifice stifles, the letter killeth, and all that," but her explanation of craft in that interview might well serve to illustrate how she bridges the chasm between formalist verse and free verse into which more than one poet has fallen, rarely with grace: ". . .it is getting the right rhythm for a particular poem, the most precise words for what I mean, . . .trying to make the poem a unified whole"(6). Form itself, then, the skeleton, the blueprint, the spider's web, makes the poem work. A poem is a contraption complicated as a Swiss clock but it's no timepiece; prosodic metrics have nothing to do with mathematics. Poems tell our time from birth to death but not by numbers.

Now I want to belabor a poem sufficiently to irritate many readers (and probably Vassar Miller too) to demonstrate how it operates, although I hasten to say at the outset that in all likelihood she is not always entirely aware of the mechanism at work. Surely prosody now

refers to whatever a poet brings to bear on the organic
honesty of a poem as well as traditional metrics and
rhymes, but Vassar Miller's own prosody does suggest a
conscious attention to the *rhythmos* of scansion's synco-
pations and to sound's own descant. "Alternatives" is
an early poem never reprinted, so far as I know, after
its initial appearance in *Adam's Footprint*:

> What will assuage this dog-self of his hunger,
> Pawing among the garbage heaps, his pang
> gouging through caverns of his guts like anger
> Denied the dignity of cause and tongue?
> Quivering beneath his gluttonies bedrocked
> In belly and in blood, the jig and jerk
> Of titillated nerves tend to obstruct
> A transcendental nuance in his bark.
> So, when he prays, his whining never bounces
> Beyond the roof of ego; should he fit
> His grunts to rhyme, a new Narcissus minces
> Before the mirror, ogling his own snout.
> Deprived of rutting, poetry, and prayer--
> He takes a nap or plays some solitaire.
>   (*AF*, p. 10)

Many of Vassar Miller's most dedicated readers are
unlikely to have even heard of "Alternatives." Copies of
Adam's Footprint are scarcer than 1623 folios or last
month's tv guide, few printed or few preserved, now
priceless for collectors or then valueless for readers
largely indifferent to most slender volumes by unknown
poets. I wish "Alternatives" had turned up in *Wage
War on Silence*, along with the other poems from
Adam's Footprint it carried. I wish it had been included
in *Selected and New Poems*. I'm glad to get it back into
print here, no major poem but a good one to begin to
chart the route Vassar Miller's prosody has taken her. It
may suggest as well, of course, several concerns in her

subsequent work in familiar images and analogies: the beast-epic in miniature; the visceral vocabulary; the self-deprecating humor; the tormenting voice of sex masquerading as appetite in rooting's savage pun on "rutting"; poetry's eloquence reduced to a "bark" by the body's urges; prayer only "whining" as it rationalizes; the escape from failure into sleep or, by devastating implication, other kinds of solitary activity; autobiography behind metaphor's domino. The "alternatives" are not so various: nothing satisfies the hunger, nothing sings in the poetry, nothing in the prayer avoids self; instead anger, the neural twitch, and delusion take over, and their substitutions reduce all "alternatives" either to the oblivion of sleep or, to put it crudely, playing with oneself physically and emotionally as well as intel lectually. "Alternatives" is remarkable for its density, for the concentration of its images, and for its disquieting disclosures no more about the poet than about the reader. But it is all the more remarkable because the "alternatives" of the title are not limited to the content. As if to reinforce the subject itself, the poem functions through a series of alternatives to its form.

The English sonnet has long been Vassar Miller's most familiar prosodic trademark, if not necessarily one she prefers, beginning here and continuing through "Love's Bitten Tongue," that twenty-two-unit *tour de force* to which I referred earlier. Pure form--categorically, I am not speaking of anything else but form itself--has never demonstrated Vassar Miller's pyrotechnics to more astonishing advantage than in "Alternatives." The conventional pattern--beginning with three independently rhymed quatrains on three differing aspects of the poem's subject--make a comfortable fit for "rutting, poetry, and prayer." Similarly, the concluding couplet allows for graceful closure, with a rhyme of its own to summarize the quatrains in a comment, a solution, an ambiguity, or sometimes as in "Alternatives" in all three. Indeed, the rhyme scheme of any English sonnet lets the reader in on progressional organization before he reads a line: abab cdcd efef gg. In this poem, composed of "alternatives," not one true end-rhyme occurs in the quatrains. As if to compile a catalog in consonance, the poem deliberately avoids them, offering instead the proximity of *hunger* and *anger*; the slant of *page* and *tongue*; the verbal accuracy an eye will deny in *bedrocked* and *obstruct*, complicated by the slant rhyme of *rock* and *ruc* while *rock* also anticipates *ob*; *jerk* and *bark*, *bounces* and *minces*, and *fit* and *snout* all consonate through vocal approximation. In each case, the appearance and the sound are "alternatives" to reinforce the "alternatives" for "rutting, poetry, and prayer." These graceful errors, I suggest, are deliberate, while the consonantal values are always pure, the voiced and unvoiced placements never false; even the voiced *d* as pronounced in *bedrocked* is unvoiced to agree with *obstruct*. Now this kind of deliberate scrutiny alarms readers and writers alike; students come away from the classroom ready for a healthy hike around the track and poets go back to their desks bemused to have learned of their own ingenuity. None of which can matter: when the act of making a poem involves rhyme, the result may be a strong thrall of form and content than in a concrete poem where the actual shape resembles the subject. Earlier on I threatened to belabor "Alternatives"; there's more. To further alter expectations in an English sonnet's rhymes, Vassar Miller incorporates two feminine pairs, and in each case she further complicates them: *hunger* and *anger* interrupted first by the apocopated *hunger* and *among*, then by *pang* and *anger*; *bounces* and *minces* interrupted by the internal *Narcissus minces*. She interlaces rhyme in *assuage* and *garbage*; she even incorporates a combined amphisbaenic rhyme and consonantal echo in *guts* and *tongue*; and she light-rhymes the quatrains through scattered present participial endings to echo the parallel cravings expressed in the poem. Not surprisingly, the closing couplet rhymes purely, but since "solitaire" must serve as poor substitute for "rutting, poetry, and prayer," it only rhymes through counter-elision: "prayer" is as easily two syllables as one. Finally, the sonnet is alive with alliterative patterns that sing to the ear out for music only, and of course any ear may hear all this long-winded blowing about "alternatives" as only music if it wants to.

I have said nothing about the images in the poem. By strict definition, metaphor is not in prosody's province; nevertheless, if prosody locks a poem into itself, it is difficult to ignore the powerful alliance between the "caverns" and "gluttonies," nor the sexual frustration in "the jig and jerk/Of titillated nerves," nor the irony in Narcissus admiring "his own snout" as he preens over his hapless verse, nor the connecting tissue of animal ravening and all too human guilt, capable of envisioning "dignity" while searching through the refuse of others for love or one or another of love's regents. In every case, the observations these images and actions imply are accusatory but oddly affectionate. As "this dog-self" is to poet's self, it is also the reader's self; no persona takes the blame. There is neither sentimentality nor smirk in the tone of "Alternatives" but instead a wry grace in its baleful stare at all of us. Tone, too, occupies prosody's territory.

Metrically, "Alternatives" is fascinating as a variation on the conventional iambic pentameters of the English sonnet. Feminine endings add additonal syllables in four lines, one of which reverses the first foot; three other lines reverse feet, one of them rightly demanding a spondee of "bedrocked" and another allowing a spondee of "own snout"--sufficient alterations to avoid the dangerous thud of the metronome in any poem brave enough today to operate in conventional metrics. Further, the poem allows for variations to approximate ordinary speech, though not without contrivance, since every line scans with five obvious beats. The lines are divided between those complete in themselves and those that spill over into the next, but in deliberate disproportion. Only five of them are acatalexic; the other nine are enjambed. Morever, none of the rhymes is a cloture, and only two might be assessed in semi-cloture. The sonnet is conversational rather than lyrical, speech rather than song, despite the arch elegance of isolated phrases and the power of its images. Unless the voice insists on caressing each line as an individual verse--a sore temptation and a viable approach to Vassar Miller's poems because of their explicit music--it is even difficult to avoid the sound of speech in "Alternatives." In parallel columns below, I have beat out the poem's metrical prosody and its metrical speech. Other scannings are doubtless possible, since we all breathe to emphasize somewhat differently. This one, read simply as a monolog of the head or the heart as well as by the voice, with full recognition of the enjambments and punctuation, is not likely to persuade many listeners they are hearing--as a metrical prosody--a rather conventional English sonnet.

./././././.	/.././/../.
/../././././	/..../..///
/../././././.	/../...////.
./././././	././..././
/..../././/	/...././..//
./././././	./..../././
./././././	./...//../
./././././	././..//./
./././././.	/../././././.
./././././	./././..
./././././.	./././//./.
./././.../	././...///
./././././/[.]	././.../.
./././././	..././//..

And to what does all this belaboring lead? An easy conviction that even the lightest explication of a poem "takes all the beauty of it out," as students learn to mouth by rote when urged to believe that poetry is an exercise in slow reading. It need not be this slow, but even when it is, all the tinkering with the contraption comes to an end, the words upon the printed page are where they were in the beginning. They have not changed at all. They say what they said before we saw them. But perhaps we have changed.

Does the belaboring lead anywhere else for Vassar Miller? I think so. If she was capable at the outset of her long love affair with poetry of writing "Alternatives," what has followed it can only induce, in one reader at least, a stunned allegiance and admiration. It is crucial, however, that she be absolved of conscious responsibility for what I find in "Alternatives," or any other poem for that matter. "A poem results frm a fusion of intellect and passion, is the fruit of their union," she said in her Hammond interview. "What makes this possible is the nature of the poem itself. A poem is not made out of ideas alone or of feeling alone. Otherwise we have essay or emoting, not poetry." (7) Similarly, with too conscious a prosody we have that Swiss clock or mere cleverness, not poetry. I dare say that much of what I find in "Alternatives" may strike its author with more than a little alarm. A poem is no garden where a pedant's footnotes grow like weeds to strangle what's planted there; a poem is some arcane combination of sweat and heart-heave, God's touch and touch-typing, drafts on foolscap and drafts in the head, familiarity with the dictionary and with "thumbing the thesaurus/of my bones." (*ICS*, p. 10) In an unpublished draft of a piece called "My Life as a Poet"--she may have used some of the material elsewhere--Vassar Miller says that, in poetry, "the *what* is the *how*. Until and unless I know how to say what I want to say, I have not said it."(8) Knowing how and saying how, of course are not the same thing, but in an astonishing number of poems that have followed "Alternatives," Vassar Miller has demonstrated an uncanny alliance between form and content, a shaping intelligence.

In the last decade or so, she has opened her poems to admit some startling experiments. In *If I Could Sleep Deeply Enough* only half a dozen of over forty poems employ rhyme in any conventional sense; there are only three sonnets, one of which is unrhymed despite some vocalic echoes. Several poems operate in three-line stanzas, sometimes in parallel syllabification, sometimes drawing tension from contradictions in line lengths, the latter especially effective in some longer poems as well. "Spastics," that grisly and compassionate assessment of common responses to people with handicaps, derives much of its strength from its grotesque images, but much strength too from the prosody of its spacing. It is difficult not to begin reading the first stanza in the middle because of the staring space following three harsh lines of two words each, in contrast to the acerbic eloquence of the first and only full-length line. Their brevity is framed by ugly alliterations in parallel. Their summary in a final line is longer on the page than they are but equally abrupt, two beats only despite the number of syllables.

> They are not beautiful, young, and strong
> / when it strikes,
> but wizened in wombs like everyone else,
> like monkeys,
> like fish,
> like worms,
> creepy-crawlies from yesterday's rocks
> tomorrow will step on.

The other two stanzas are less symmetrical only in
lacking the framing alliterative phrases in the first,
although the repetition of "No one" in the second and
the interlacing "rarely marry" and "really make" in the
third are sufficiently telling parallels.

> Hence presidents, and most parents, don't
>   / have to worry
> No one in congress will die of it. No one else.
> Don't worry.
> They just
> hang on
> drooling, stupid from watching too much TV,
> born-that-way senile,
>
> rarely marry, expected to make it with Jesus,
> never really make it at all,
> don't know how,
> some can't
> feed themselves,
> fool with, *well*--Even some sappy saint said they
> look young because pure.
>
> <div align="right">(<i>ICS</i>, p. 39)</div>

The sardonic double-readings, the slangy gallows humor,
the progressive short-hand in sentence structure all
serve well as prosodic devices here; more formally, in a
devastating parimion, so does that "sappy saint," a
creepy-crawly with a rock all his own.

In subsequent poems, Vassar Miller's prosodies have
ranged widely. If the open tercet has preoccupied her,
she has experimented as well with variations on Japan-
ese katuata and haiku, even her own version of the
mondo. There is always some danger in the latter
coming off like something out of a fortune cookie, Jap-
anese being about as alien to Chinese as it is to
English, emotionally at least. But two of these, from

"An Essay in Criticism by Way of Rebuttal" in *Selected and New Poems*, are handsomely turned in their economy and, read aloud, their music marks their prosody as well as their poetry:

> Every descent into silence is
> the risk of never returning.
>
> Every tentative word is
> in peril of being wanting.

(SNP, p. 155)

The various prosodies in *Approaching .Nada*, Vassar Miller's long meditation on time and faith, poetry and history, is itself rich enough in extravagance and risk to double these observations. Elsewhere, she has written blank verse, open verse; dramatic monologs; villanelles and pantoums; serious doggerel guaranteeing laughter; blasphemous prayers pious as a psalm; and I would not be surprised to learn she has tried her hand at the French kyrielle or the Welsh rhupunt. Just as if to prove she could do it, she turned out those twenty-two heroic achievements in both prosody and poetry, "Love's Bitten Tongue." If, in their three hundred-eight lines (!), an occasional flat note or careless chord sounds, the brilliance of total performance is sufficiently dazzling. It always is, because her prosody gives her poetry its integrity; that, and because in every one of her poems she tells me what I need to hear when my pedantry threatens to get in the way of what poetry, finally, is about, perhaps best expressed in "Or as Gertrude Stein Says. . ." from *My Bones Being Wiser*:

> When the sky is as blue as itself,
> and the tree is as green as its leaves--
> a poem is only
> taking a child's downy skull

gently between your hands
and, with not so much breath as might startle
        / a gnat's wing,
whispering,
"Look!"

(MB, p. 42)

Passionate Scriptures of the Body

ROBERT BONAZZI

Vassar Miller's poetry is a balance of form and ravaged form; a tension between the aesthetic body of the poem and the tortured body of reality.

In an early poem from her second book, *Wage War on Silence*, Miller published a prototypic text of her thematic concerns. The cascading monologue of "Offering: For All My Loves" is a twenty-two line sentence personified as a vessel. The voice of the vessel offers itself ("This vessel take--"), and then compares its shape to a litany of more aesthetic things.

> No chalice and no goblet,
> Nothing so picturesque as a gourd
> Or an oaken bucket,
> But more like a rusty can
> Kicked up from the dirt
>
> (*SNP*, p. 27)

Miller chooses her comparisons carefully. The vessel is not a Christian chalice nor an aristocratic goblet; it is not as picturesque as an old peasant gourd nor even a modest oaken bucket. Rather, it is the ravaged form of "a rusty can," evoking the poet's own tortured body forced into is conforming clothing, a child "Buckled and bent and warped" like an abandoned object.

Throughout her work, Miller invents a rich variety of images for the rejected body. In "Slump" she writes:

> The body, God knows why, creeps
> along, some crazy creature
> half an insect, half a tumbleweed.   (*SNP*, p. 83)

This calls Kafka to mind. Not just "The Metamorphosis," which is truly this poet's evolving form, but also Kafka's notion of *smallness*. As Kafka wrote in his book-length letter, *Dearest Father* (1), there are:

> Two possibilities: making oneself infinitely small or being so. The second is perfection, that is to say, inactivity, the first is beginning, that is to say, action.

Miller's version of *smallness* in her early books is that of action, whereas Kafka's ideal was inactivity, being at one with the all.

In "Subterfuge" she writes of her father, who gives her a typewriter as a gift. He enters the poem

> bearing it in his arms like an awkward bouquet
>
> for his spastic child who sits down
> on the floor, one knee on the frame
> of the typewriter, and holding her left wrist
>
> with her right hand, in that precision known
> to the crippled, pecks at the keys
> with a sparrow's preoccupation.
>
> (*SNP*, p. 131)

Again, the diminutive figure who, "Falling by chance on rhyme," and "pretending pretense and playing at playing" realizes that her fun is "a delaying action against what she knows," "as she toils at tomorrow, tensed at her makeshift toy."

Even though it's a tentative beginning, the crippled child takes up language "in that precision known/to the crippled" as an instrument of transformation. The child, like the "hunk of corroded tin" in "Offering: For All My Loves," will endure and prevail because they are:

Yet filled with the liquor of lightning,
The same as distilled from the flowers
/ of children,
From the arbors of home,
From the wild grapes of martyrs, trampled
/ for Christ,
Or as mixed with the solder of music,
With the webwax of words,
The same and no different,
Only shaped to misshapenness

(*SNP*, p. 27)

The child and the vessel are like · the martyrs (or various "innocents" Miller depicts) who are "trampled for Christ," and in him find they are "The same and no different," yet "shaped to misshapenness." The poet juxtaposes the philosophical acceptance of the ravaged form with the human bitterness at how this body is mis-read by others. At this point in "Offering: For All My Loves," the offering becomes a warning.

Hold me with care and decorum
For a little but not too long
Lest my jagged edge cut you,
My acrid drip scald you,
Etching a crooked shadow
On the lip of your proper love.

(*SNP*, p. 27)

She knows her God will accept any transcription of her body, but the "proper love" of humans will recoil from that "crooked shadow."

Vassar Miller entered the garden of poetry as a child in the title poem to her first book, *Adam's Footprint*. There she discovers her first step of experience, a primal image on the floor of Eden. Yet she knows that

> The foot of Adam leaves the mark
> Of some child scrabbling in the dark.
>
> (*SNP*, p. 13)

Adam's signature is that of the child in a new world, a world which must be named and learned. Like Adam, the poet is a child of wonder, passion and paradox. But she will not accept the fate of the "Spastic Child" (*SNP*, p. 14), whose mind is a "bright bird, forever trapped in silence." The footprint, like the trapped mind, is the silenced body.

In "Without Ceremony," Miller writes that

> We find ourselves where tongues cannot
> / wage war
> On silence (farther, mystics never flew)
> But on the common wings of what we are,
> Borne on the wings of what we bear,
> / toward You,
> Oh word, in whom our wordiness dissolves,
> When we have not a prayer except ourselves.
>
> (*SNP*, p. 25)

In her third book, *My Bones Being Wiser*, her experiental research returns to the body--this time as silent prayer. The title poem, aptly subtitled "A Eucharistic Meditation"--or a meditation upon the transcended body of Christ--begins

> At Thy Word
> my mind may wander
> but my bones worship
> beneath the dark waters of my blood
> whose scavenger fish
> have picked them clean.
>
> (*SNP*, p. 60)

Again, the bones--picked clean--openly offer their blank text for the imprint of God.

In "Loneliness" Miller replaces Adam's footprint with God's.

> This silence, this crying,
> O my God, is my country
> with Yours the sole footstep besides my own.
> Save me amid its landscapes
> so terrible, strange
> I am almost in love with them!
>
> (*SNP*, p. 43)

Rather than waging war on silence, the bones being wiser *become silence*, and the poet touches the ineffable within. It is in this "country" that the paradoxes resolve into the One. Silence is crying and "wordiness dissolves" into the word: *Yes*. It is in the silent music that the poet hears her "Belated Lullaby":

> Where flesh and spirit dance,
> Shadowing, bound yet free
> Bach's ordered ecstasy.
>
> (*SNP*, p. 48)

Yet, it that temporal space of the body, she writes, in "A Bird in the Hand," that

> I do not feel the peace of the saints,
> light fusing with darkness,
> passing all understanding.
>
> (*SNP*, p. 58)

Except for certain instants of ecstasy, the poet vividly feels the body's sensate cage. Whereas the mystic transcends the body's text, Miller grapples with it. Whereas the mystic writes an ineffable incantation of silence, Miller's deeply religious verse measures its music and clarifies its meaning.

In her poem, "A Dream from the Dark Night"-- based on an anecdote of St. John burning the letters of St. Teresa--Miller finds herself in "the desert of dark- ness/where Your silence speaks so loud/I cannot hear You." (*SNP*, p. 62) At the point of ecstatic trans- cendence, the mystic becomes silent spirit, while the poet returns to the flesh. Vassar Miller's scriptures reach toward that transcendence, then become a painful and beautiful reshaping of experience into poetry.

In Miller's "Introduction to a Poetry Reading," the body becomes her living text. She tells us she was

> born with my mod dress sewn into my body
> stitched to my flesh,
> basted into my bones.
> I could never, somehow, take it all off
> to wash the radical dirt out.
>
> (*SNP*, p. 87)

Her tone is not apologetic but defiant. The poem concludes with nearly the same warning as "Offering: For All My Loves":

> So, bear me
> as I bear you,
> high, in the grace of greeting.
>
> (*SNP*, p. 87)

Too radical, she is forced back into her own body. The same retreat occurs in several other poems from *If I Could Sleep Deeply Enough*, her darkest and most naked book. From "Tired" comes the book's title and another variation on body's language.

> If I could

sleep deeply enough,
I might touch the eye
of dark, life.

Yet the way
I sleep, men drink salt.
Always wearier
upon waking--

I have written
these lines without book,
thumbing the thesaurus
of my bones.

(*SNP*, p. 95)

Her very bones, that inner text of the body, defiantly
thumb their own variations and break the skin of form.
 Miller's "Insomniac's Prayer" is a portrait of a
"body knotted into a fist/clenching against itself," and
she plaintively asks, "Oh, who will unsnarl my body/
into gestures of love?" Will it be her lover, her God, or
death?

Who will nudge the dreams back
   / into my head,
back into my bones, where rhyming
   / with one another
like wind chimes,
they will make music whenever I move?

(*SNP*, p. 90)

These are poems of silenced music, broken open by
despair. "Read my face and my hands," she tells us in
"Fantasia," "stripped raw like Jesus"--or the body
sanctified by pain.
 In "Posthumous Letter to Thomas Merton" Miller
finds her ideal counterpart. A poet of equally intense

spirituality, Merton's work reflects a similar reading of the liturgy, theology, and the lives of the saints and mystics. Both poets were labeled superficially as "religious" poets in their earlier books, and then virtually ignored once their work opened in form and intimacy. Miller ends her letter ("less poem than presumption") with a long interrogatory that could stand as her poetics. Never pious, and never certain, the poet continues to ask the philosophical questions.

> I ask you, self-styled marginal man,
> Does not each sufferer always inhabit
> The edges of the world as pioneer
> To prove how much humanity can bear
> And still be human, experimenter in
> The bloody laboratory of our lives.
> Taking and testing every pain tossed from
> The cosmos, fragments we reshape,
> As best as the materials allow,
> To buttress God's cathedrals built from chaos?
>
> (*SNP*, p. 2)

Vassar Miller's question for Merton--for all poets, and for God--is answered in her definition of poetry.

> Poetry is creative in that it makes an artifact where none was before, only a mass of thoughts and emotions and sensations; it is redemptive, since it makes art out of non-art, something of beauty and value; it is sanctifying in that it confers order upon chaos. These three functions are one. (2)

Miller has accepted, mastered and broken the forms poetry has given her--from Hopkins, Robinson and Dickinson toward the poets of the nada. She has woven the question into the fabric in the manner of a skeptical philosopher. She has reshaped intense experience into passionate scriptures of the body. Vassar Miller and poetry and her loving knowledge of God are one, a trinity joined in the soul.

In her 133-line poem in open form, the chapbook *Approaching Nada*, Miller asks the Abbot of the French Academy and the concept of "Pure Poetry," what he means by his statement, "Le poete, c'est un mystique manque," and then speculates upon his words.

> An aborted mystic,
> a frustrated mystic,
> or did you mean,
> simply, a sorry one?
> Doubtless the latter, since
> the poet like the mouse will scuttle
> clean to the border
> of the ineffable,
> then scurry back
> with tidbits of the Vision.
>
> (*SNP*, p. 120)

Her poems are "tidbits of the Vision," appropriate to the diminutive nature of the poet as mouse scuttling, or as "child scrabbling" ("Adam's Footprint"), or as "the meanest grub/struggling to swim on concrete." (*SSC*, p. 12). These utterings are not like those of the mystics, who "leap once and for all/headlong into darkness." Miller is not one of "These poets of the Nada." Rather, she is like Robinson, who said that "Poetry is trying to say what cannot be said." (3) Miller is a poet who, in *Approaching Nada*, becomes one of the "mystics of/the bruising thing," who "climb up bloody concretes/to leave nailed high/white pieces of themselves." Like Christ, who gave up his body for the Word, the poet offers the body of the poem as sacrifice. In this

powerful work, where Miller does finally "take it all off/
to wash the radical dirt out," she discovers that place
"Somewhere between silence and ceremony" (as yet
unfound in the earlier "Without Ceremony"), wherefrom
"springs the Word,' God's *Yes* given to the poet. It is
the selfsame word, that subtle ascent toward silence,
which is

> the wellhead of all hush feeding the roots
> of tongues, whether of men or angels, interchange
> between us and Your world. Listen, whoever
> tunes an ear.
>
> (*SNP*, p. 123)

She listens, yet her faith is "fired by doubt," and
her "wings clipped by busy book and body, still in
You,/my Phoenix!" It is only through her "Phoenix,"
that "Sweet bird of Christmas," that she can rise from
the ashes of her body. Otherwise, she is grounded by
her "busy book and body," the limiting forms of flesh
and intellect. No longer can she be "content with the
pseudonym/of my name, with the disguise/provided by
my body," for she must be "awakened astonished in
the streets/of my identity" ("Encounter," *SNP*, p. 107).
As she approaches nada, that dark hemisphere bound as
one with the hemisphere of light, she knows that

> Every poet knows
> what the saint knows
>
> that every new day is
> to retake the frontier of one's name.
>
> (*SNP*, p. 155)

The difference between the poet--even a mystical,
Edenic poet like Vassar Miller--and a true mystic, is
that the poet names what he or she loves, and the

mystic erases all identity. The poet enters that great silence in order to return to the senses with words for it, shaped into fragments "As best as the materials allow."

For the mystic, "mysticism is no isolated vision, no fugitive glimpse of reality, but a complete system of life. . . .It is the name of that organic process which involves the perfect consummation of the Love of God," wrote Evelyn Underwood in her seminal study of the phenomena of mysticism. (4)

Miller's subject is not mysticism nor the luminous nada, but the search for these realms in poetic terms. It is this very searching which is her subject, both in life and in poetry. The same is true of Dickinson and Merton--all "mystics of/the bruising thing"--the body, that vessel of identity, which becomes "The bloody laboratory of our lives." (*SNP*, p. 3)

While the mystic is gradually purified, illuminated and transformed from the very roots of being, the poet, a "Middling-good ghost," moves inwardly toward "roots of shifted waters/shifting toward nada." This activity moves though the passionate experiences triggered by creative intuition, sensory pleasures, birthing and dying, prayer and meditation, "altered states of consciousness," and nature itself. These and other "peak experiences" are the secondary mystical phenomena--essential to all poetry, but transcended by true mysticism.

Even with the breaking of form and the "roots of shifted waters" in *Approaching Nada*, the poet is yet that organic form of the body. Again, there is the search, as the poet wanders

> down hallways of my body, ghost
> prowling passages of my blood
> to my most hidden corners

where "still/I know my name." (*SNP*, p. 126)

All these themes--from *Adam's Footprint* to *Approaching Nada*--form a beautiful arc from innocence through experience to a second innocence. Those early books, so lathered with a distant fear, become washed with wisdom in *Appraoching Nada*. While "The foot of Adam leaves its mark/Of some child scrabbling in the dark" in her first book, she is willing yet to "trace footprints/of princes, rebels, martyrs"--all images for Christ--two decades later in *Approaching Nada*. It is this courageous tracing which signifies Vassar Miller as a new child in the wilderness of the psyche. And it is the grace of her finest forms that make her a poet of the first order in contemporary American poetry.

Vassar Miller's Anatomy of Silence

SISTER BERNETTA QUINN

Few words in the English language have such magnetic connotations as silence, an advantage writers know: Robert Bly, *Silence in the Snowy Fields*; Morton T. Kelsey, *The Other Side of Silence*. Michael Endo's *Silence*, a novel about two priests in early Japan whose compassion for peasant-victims of persecution led them to defect, symbolizes in its title God's non-response to their dilemma over divided loyalties; the author's choice of silence as metaphor indicates the ambivalence at the heart of the term, an ambivalence prominent in the nine books of poetry by Vassar Miller, most particularly in her 1960 *Wage War on Silence*. Throughout her work this artist has both attacked and espoused silence, considering it sometimes as an enemy but then again as a refuge, a source of beauty (for example, the image of cicadas mowing the "thick grass of silence" in "View from a Small Garden" and the same insects serving as the voice of silence in "Song for a Summer Afternoon"). So omnipresent is the noun that analyzing Miller's use of it may well provide insight into her development over forty years, during a distinguished literary career. Strangely enough, though for a quarter of a century she has enjoyed a reputation as an excellent religious lyricist, almost no criticism of her work has appeared.

Many practitioners of poetry have tried to describe the poet's job; Vassar Miller, alternate poet-laureate of Texas in 1963, contributes such an attempt on the dustjacket of her first volume in the Wesleyan Poetry Program: "The title of *Wage War on Silence* reflects my conviction that poetry, indeed all art, is the striving to say the unsayable, to express the inexpressible." These four words occur in the middle of the opening sonnet, "Without Ceremony," which is given a section all to itself. As is the case in a very large number of her poems, she is addressing God:

> We find ourselves where tongues
> / cannot wage war
> On silence (farther, mystics never flew)
> But on the common wings of what we are,
> Borne on the wings of what we bear,
> / toward You,
> Oh Word, in whom our wordiness dissolves,
> When we have not a prayer except ourselves.
>
> (*WW*, p. 3)

In this miniature "essay in criticism," prayer rather than art is really the subject, though (and rightly) she considers prayer as an art. Wordlessness here seems an inevitable and indeed a desirable state. Yet as writer Miller knows she must neither court nor even accept silence, but rather conquer it, as she has been endeavoring to do since that first Hopkinsesque poem at eight meant for her mother. (1) Convinced of the value of transmuting transient life into permanent artifact, also of striving to effect communication between personas as well as with God, she mirrors this enormous double challenge in the more recent title, *Struggling to Swim on Concrete*; Jane Cooper, reviewing *Onions and Roses*, suggests as much when she speaks of Miller's battle against silence as "the solitary struggle of conscience with language, the attempt to achieve a genuine personal voice." (2)

Howard Nemerov in his anthology *Poets on Poetry* presents one of the rare autobiographical statements Vassar Miller has made to date; she is as reluctant to issue these as was Randall Jarrell. To his interview question "What is a poet?" she offers this comment about her poetics as related to the naming of her second collection:

> But the phrase suggests the very nature of poetry, which is war waged with the silence of misunderstanding between men, with the silence of God that Christ endured on the cross, summing up in Himself our individual endurance. One critic protested that "Wage War on Silence" is an awkward title, but waging war on silence is an awkward thing to do. (3)

In the same book "The Resolution" shows how successfully this frail Texan woman, afflicted with cerebral palsy since birth and now in her sixties, has carried on that warfare. It is based on the *why* that Jesus addressed to his Father on Calvary, "My God, my God, why have you forsaken me?"; she and the Lord, at first fencers, become in the end dancers; then as the metaphor shifts, their mutual why is a candle in the sconce of God's response.

Yeats once wrote, "I have poured my life into my poems as if into a mold." To some extent, all poets do that, making their work a leading source of information as to character, personality. Much of Vassar Miller's poetry stresses silence as functioning in interpersonal relationships, revelatory of the sort of individual she is (and how appositely that noun *individual* is used in her case)! Though many of her pieces are specifically inscribed to friends and relatives, others, such as "Eden Revisited," are not. The first part is apparently unrelated to the second, about a leaf given her mother in 1912 by a friend named Helen; yet the sections are united through the title, in that the two paradises are transitory. For Vassar Miller, once the Eden of free confidences is over, silence becomes a secure haven;

gone are the days of innocence when she and her
unnamed companion, as the epigraph promises, can talk
all night through. Now, confronted by Judge Life, she is
defended by the lawyer, Silence: "words were my
lawyers once before Judge Life./Now when he passes
sentence,/silence and I stand side by side." (SSC, p. 50)
She has learned her lesson, having been "more times
than one" thrown into jail for passing counterfeit statements, comparable to phony bills. That the lyric is
grouped among those in *Struggling to Swim on Concrete*
seems fitting.

   "The Tree of Silence," intended for Nancy, goes a
bit further in its euology of a virtue spoken of here in
terms of a tree, the roots of which stand for divine as
well as human dialogue. Like apples "pinched" and
"wan," doomed to become windfalls are the words of
Vassar and Nancy exchanged in their carefree season
("Upon the branches of our silence hang our words,/
Half-ripened fruit. . . .") Miller the philosopher continues
to merge their plight with the human condition: "For
when was language ever food for human yearning!"
Equating words with"Sun-gilded rain/Mocking the sheen
of golden peach," she sadly concludes that they "only
drain/Hearts of strength" and confides their friendship
to prayer, the art which life itself, though the way be
"long and lonely," will teach them. (WW, p. 51)

   Some of Vassar Miller's lyrics go so far as to extol
silence as beatitude: "Conquered" and "Unnecessary"
are such, though included in the collection (*Wage War
on Silence*) which gives a pejorative sense to the noun.
In the most felicitous relationship communication exists
without and beyond language, which the second of these
calls quite unnecessary for understanding. Before the
advent of the visitor in this lyric, the poet plans their
conversation, but when the other arrives Vassar Miller
expresses only confusion, through the homely similes
she handles so well:

With your coming
the words I have arranged
stumble like year-old children,
my thoughts scattered
like flustered pullets.

(*WW*, p. 65)

In quietness her friend answers the questions there is really no need to answer, any more than "to beg/the earth to turn/Or God to be." As Father William Johnston, S.J., says in *Silent Music*: "When two people begin to love, they may chatter and use words a good deal; but as their intimacy grows, words become less necessary and are even superfluous." (4) From the gathering *My Bones Being Wiser*, "In Love" says much the same thing: "You do not move to music,/yet in your presence sit my bones/singing in silence." (*MB*, p. 35)

"Conquered," which adjoins "Unnecessary" in *Wage War on Silence*, is probably to the same person, to whom the poet attributes such gentleness that her own thoughts become children sitting around the other as if in a school setting, or flowers "wilting and waiting/the dews" of the friend's attention. The conclusion is soothing, contemplative as a minor-keyed Mozart violin concerto:

For you do not wound my silence
with a sound,
but beyond word or act
bless me in your being.

(*WW*, p. 65)

The children figure of speech occurs again in "Each After Its Own Kind": "I keep still/like a child/sitting upon the floor,/waiting." (*MB*, p. 36)

In contrast, "The Logic of Silence" portrays a love affair wherein silence is the gloomy anticlimax of what was once beautiful, in a time when the poet's heart can be described as "Melting to music in the palm of the lover who has discovered her attraction to him; this image changes in the second stanza to foaming waters, used also to characterize her mind in its quick alterations. The final eight lines attempt to disclose the significance of the title, but here that seventeenth-century idiom of George Herbert, to whom Jean Gould has likened Vassar Miller, (5) strikes one as oppressive: making sense out of the conclusion is if not impossible at least difficult:

> Now I move heavily
> To that tune
> Teased with its words
> Whose splintered chips
> Massed by its tide
> Into the bone
> Deadlock love's weight
> Against my lips.
>
> (*WW*, p. 57)

Words like *splintered* (in the context, symbolic of a broken heart) and *deadlock*, *padlock*, imply a collapsed relationship; however, the exigencies of rhyme tend to force the thought.

"Carmel: Impression" in the same volume takes an opposite point of view by preferring silence to sound, blaming man for interference in the sublime seascape: "For his language has sullied the sheen/Of silence like the storm-eagle's croak." (*WW*, p. 56) "Loneliness" pursues this geographical emphasis in its extensive anatomizing of silence:

> So deep is this silence
> that the insects, the birds,
> the talk of the neighbors in the distance,

the whir of the traffic, the music
are only its voices
and do not contradict it.

so deep is this crying
that the silence, the hush,
the quiet, the stillness, the not speaking,
the never hearing a word
are only the surge
of its innumerable waters.

This silence, this crying,
O my God, is my country
With Yours the sole footstep beside my own.
Save me amid its landscapes
So terrible strange,
I am almost in love with them!

(*WW*, p. 130)

The scene is an actual one, perhaps the front porch of
Vassar Miller's home on Vassar Street in Houston. To
comprehend the lyric, the reader can best find guidance
in its title, "Loneliness": the interior landscapes, those
of the country of Silence, are shared only with God;
frightening as they are, the poet loves, or almost loves
them, just as Gerard Manley Hopkins, with Robinson
and Herbert a strong influence on her early Muse, loves
his "cliffs of fall" in the dark sonnets. The synonym for
silence in stanza two, *hush*, is a noun Miller likes, using
it in "Resolve" as exchangeable with "absence of
noise" and in a masterstroke of imagery in "Easter
Eve: A Fantasy": "The bowl of hush held lifted to the
the first bird's trilling." (*MB*, p. 48)

In Vassar Miller, silence is often related to death, as
Shelley relates it in "Fragment: To Silence": "Oh well
are Death and Sleep and Thou/Three brethren named,"
and as Shakespeare does in Hamlet' "The rest is

silence." "Unspoken Dialogue" tells of a frozen mute-
ness become permanent because of the death of the
addressee: "Death having cleaved our shell/Of Silence,
silence was our core as well," the chiasmus revealing
an incompatibility which would have been shattering,
even if words could have connected the two. The pain of
the closing brings up the reader sharply: "For in heart's
tongue-tied lull/The word unspoken proves unspeakable" (*WW*, p. 19) In the blank verse letter to Thomas
Merton with which she prefaces *Selected and New
Poems 1950-1980*, "Now that your words have smoked
away to silence" seems a lament for the dumbness
wrought by death. "Leave-Taking" complains to the
dead, a loneliness that has stolen from Miller not only
the chatter but "even the silence." In "Letter to Friends
Dead and Living" she writes in rage, "sitting in silence,"
bitterly reproached by ghosts of those forever barred
from poem-making.

The *momento mori* strain that plays through the bulk
of lyric poetry frequently informs Miller's poetry. "Birthday Card to Myself" expresses a strange wish for such
an occasion, phrased in imagery reminiscent of Jarrell's
"Field and Forest," in which a farmer removes false
teeth, spectacles, even his thoughts, and finally the
world itself; in Miller, the "I" longs to discard her
history like a sweater or blouse; her past like a coat;
her minutes like stockings; even her family and her
name so that "fatherless as the leaves" she can "join
the mute ceremony of stones,/The speechless celebrations of grasses." (*SSC*, p. 29) It is as if the poet
projects herself into a future when flesh will have gone
back to the earth; the birthday is an ominous warning
that she tries to steal past barefoot.

In waging war on silence there is always the danger
that a truce may turn into a defeat and silence win. The
short poem with a very long title "An Essay in Criticism
by Way of Rebuttal" is actually on the subject of the

failure of inspiration such as haunted Randall Jarrell in those dry periods when he turned to translations, periods which he was never sure would come to an end. Miller's lyric begins:

> Every white page is
> the threat of infinite snow.
>
> Every descent into silence is
> the risk of never returning.
>
> (*SNP*, p. 155)

A similar idea occurs in "Dry Season," where "mute birds on thorny boughs of silence" represent her thoughts.

In answering Nemerov's questions for *Poets on Poetry*, Miller discriminates between religious and poetic fascination with silence: "The mystic, Bremond explains, beholds the ineffable vision and it lures him over the threshold of silence. Whereas the poet takes a quick peek and scurries back while there is still time to tell what he has glimpsed." (6) "Approaching Nada" puts Bremond's explanation into verse:

> Abbe Bremond, you wrote
> "Le poete, c'est un mystique manque."
> An aborted mystic,
> a frustrated mystic,
> or did you mean,
> simply, a sorry one?
> Doubtless the latter, since
> the poet like the mouse will scuttle
> clean to the border
> of the ineffable,
> then scurry back
> with tidbits of the Vision.   (*SNP*, p. 124)

Clearly, Miller is attracted to mystical experience, as shown in her poem "A Dream from the Dark Night," introduced by a passage from Marcelle Auclair's *Teresa of Avila* describing how John of the Cross, as the sacrifice of his last attachment, burned St. Teresa's letters.

None of Miller's poems is more powerful than this flash of vision (dream, she calls it) penetrating her own prayer life, framed between silences, producing what appears separation at first but is more apt to be union:

> Sometimes when the silence howls in my head
> till I can hear nothing else,
> when it would drown out discourse and music
> (were I suffered to hear them)
> here in the swirling sand dunes
> where the only word spoken
> cries at the quick of the heart,
> where images, mind's alabaster and ivory
> blow away into dust--
> her script as rare as a necklace of ash,
> fine as a lizard's footprint,
> vital as tendrils veining white walls of her cells
> I remember as one sucks a stone
> and so take them and burn them
> while I turn to You, O my God, my bruised feet
> leaping the meadows of Your flesh
> to the desert of darkness
> where Your silence speaks so loud
> I cannot hear You.
>
> (*SNP*, p. 62)

The poem is a dramatic monologue, or perhaps an interior one, since whether or not the companion of John of the Cross in Auclair is present is not clear. Yet somehow the "bruised feet," the howling silence, the thirst implied in sucking a stone seem Miller's own. Her unsurpassed gift for constructing original similies and metaphors is well employed to render into sense detail the saint's handwriting as St. John gazes on it for a final time: "rare as a necklace of ash,/fine as a lizard's footprint,/vital as tendrils veining white walls of her cells." (*SNP*, p. 62) Blessed Jan Van Ruysbroek in *The Spiritual Espousals* refers to such peace: "This is the dark silence in which all lovers are lost." (7) What he has in mind could perhaps be equated with her 1975 book-title *If I Could Sleep Deeply Enough*. It is a peace parallel to but unlike the peace which enwraps the dead, "who have drifted/beyond stir and stillness," as "A Bird in the Hand" puts it. Interwoven with such peace is agony:

> Mine, the catching of breath after pain,
> the peace of those who have
> almost died and still live.
>
> I pray that the peace of God fall upon me;
> the dead's comes unprayed;
> but, for now, this suffices.
>
> (*SNP*, p. 58)

As is customary in the South (in Alabama, for instance, only 2% are Catholic), Miller's views are firmly within the Protestant tradition; she is listed as Episcopalian in *Contemporary Authors*. A few of her poems, however, such as "Enlightened Selfishness," are set in Quaker meetings. In this lyric the poet is both repelled and drawn by the silence wherein friends pray. She complains about the difficulty of joining in: "A nail is driving me down/into my own silence," and later: "My silence tingles, murks up/its pristine waters." For some inexplicable reason she feels frightened. The piece is a follow-up to "Confession at a Friend's Meeting," (e.g., "From an Old Maid," "Bout with Burning") where water, as frequently happens in Miller, represents silence: "Thoughts paddle in the floods of silence" is a metaphor minus the uncomfortable connotations of certain words in the "second confession" (*nail, tingles, murks up*). Miller's recollections of Quaker worship in these two correspond with what the Jesuit George A. Maloney says in *The Silence of Surrendering Love* about a modern German classic: "Siddhartha in Hermann Hesse's novel learns the secret of life by listening to the ancient but ever new river speaking to him." (8)

The most developed and revealing exposition of Miller's interior life is the series of twenty-two sonnets called "Love's Bitten Tongue," dedicated to her nephew, Christopher. The fourteenth line throughout becomes the first one of the successor, giving the sequence a continuity. From the very start, an intimacy with Christ comes through, consonant with what she declares in the Nemerov book: "For Christianity is the religion of the Word-made-flesh and poetry is its most natural voice." (9) "Love's Bitten Tongue" opens with a prayer--direct, urgent, mostly in monosyllables: "Lord, hush this ego as one stops a bell/Clanging, cupping it softly in the palm./Should it make music, silence it as well. . ." What might be regarded as consolation, music, she now considers "a false haitus/Which brings those moments I name prayer to grief." The following passage, apart from its anachronistic typewriter, might be Emily Dickinson:

> Reality, praise seated in a chair,
> Is sweet as any lauds a church may utter,
> And my typewriter ticks a better prayer
> Than does, except by chance, my pious stutter
> Half faking faith and hope and,
> / God knows, love. . .

(SSC, p. 68)

With the sixth sonnet Miller begins to meditate specifically on her Lord Jesus Christ, whom she entreats for mercy, pleading her "puny body" and fear of death. She believes Him her partner in suffering:

> Stranger to Yourself, forever an orphan,
> Calling God Father because you were lonely,
> Riding the heave of my planet, sea-urchin,
> The sound of Your splash echoed thinly
> As mine among the galaxies clustered
> Uncanny coral reefs smothering thought
> And peeled down at last to a body blistered,
> Bared to be needled by sun. . .

> (*SSC*, p. 71)

Christ is her "poor Brother." Not until the tenth sonnet (one of the best) does the title for the sequence appear, in the concluding line, "You, my God, lonesome man, Love's bitten tongue."

Although the resemblance which Miller likes to see between herself and Flannery O'Conner (cf her sonnet "Affinity") is debatable, in this eleventh sonnet such a likeness does exist:

> Heaven's incredible wound, You who made
> This world split in half, Your birth
> / bade me hand
> As a Texas child on edge in my bed
> All Christmas Eve between waking and sleeping
> Waiting to find out what mystery broke
> In sounds more melodious than sleighbells
> / sweeping
> Over my roof. . . .

> (*SSC*, p. 72)

As she brings out in her critical writings, the fiction writer would most definitely agree that the birth of

Jesus is the midpoint of Space and Time, splitting the world in half. Significantly, Christmas occupies a large share of Miller's devotional life, second only to the Passion; here she links the "Sweet silent night" through the last line to the twelfth sonnet: "For Your cradle between greed and Your grace/Shadows Your Cross," running over the feast of Christmas into the thirteenth poem as "The melting parable of incarnation," a story about which she allows her wit to flicker in ". . .Your silence/Housing my mind to be housed in my heart,/Or rather housing heart and mind in balance," a not especially happy vestige of her love for Hopkins.

The fifteenth sonnet returns to Christmas in "You have come straying,/Ignorant Baby newborn Christmas night," after which she traces the Gospel narrative of Christ's life on earth right up to the Resurrection, ending "Love's Bitten Tongue," with her question, "What shall I do?" echoing Paul's en route to Damascus.

Christmas, as a matter of fact, furnishes the subject matter for an astonishing number of Miller's lyrics, even more than it does for Jarrell's. Among these are "In the Fullness of Time," "Lullaby After Christmas," "Bethlehem Outcast," "Ballad of the Unmiraculous Miracle," "Christmas Mourning," "Carol of Brother Ass," "Exorcism," "Post-Christmas Prayer," "Oh Hanukkah," "The Inescapable Day," "December Afternoon," "Christmas in Dark Times." Preparatory to its celebration is "In Quiet Neighborhoods," based upon the Collect for the Fourth Sunday in Advent; placed between excoriations of "progress," these lines turn the sound of the Texas wind on a rainy night into a paean of welcome for the Child:

> Now that the darkness swells with grace
> / and judgment,
> menace and mercy wrestling on the wind

risen with leaves and rain like buoyant banners
stitched with the name higher than every name,
muffled hosannahs hailing true Son of God,
true Son of our shuddering flesh--He makes
our hearts all night seeded with light rejoice.

(*SSC*, p. 47)

But often the Nativity, as in Frederic Faber and
other Catholic theologians, is associated with the Paschal
mystery: the Passion, death and Resurrection of Jesus.
Such a poem, in its undercurrents at least, is "In the
Fullness of Time," from *Wage War on Silence*, though
at first reading it seems more akin to the medieval song
"He came also still/Where his mother lay. . ." The
poignant monologue might be from Mary's lips: by the
angel. Its homespun diction is more devout than any
archaic or elevated language:

Singled out, and one of many,
I have paid the selfsame debt
Of a princess frail for bearing
Of a field hand tumbled down.
I am as common as a penny,
Costly as a coronet. . . .

Pangs of glory soon must dig
Through my yielding bone their furrow
Depth of which can never measure
What I have to cultivate--

(*WW*, p. 15)

The poem ends by repeating the line with which it
began: "I am heavy with my wait." Written in trochaic
tetrameter, rhymed *abcd* throughout, its musical quality
makes it almost a carol.

Vassar Miller is *l'etranger* named in the title of
"Bethlehem Outcast," crouching in the cold stable near

the manger, the north wind shrilling, the stench reaching her from where the oxen have fouled the floor. Through the stable door come "the gutterals of shepherds" and "singing star-bursts from the hills." The poem seems an exemplification of the way of prayer proposed by Saint Ignatius, wherein by the use of the imagination the person meditating becomes a part of an episode in the Biblical scene being contemplated:

> Those employing the Ignatian method of prayer strive to participate in the actual event by projecting themselves back into the historical happening. . . .For example, St. Ignatius in the contemplation on the Nativity of Jesus in the *Spiritual Exercises* suggests: 'I will make myself a poor, little, unworthy servant, and as though present, look upon them, contemplate them, and serve them in their needs with all possible homage and reverence. (10)

Written in the villanelle form, "Bethlehem Outcast" shows the "I" watching the Magi offer gifts, herself a "wiseman without winter lore," a "bumpkin naked to the cold that kills!"

If Miller's work taken as a whole did not prove otherwise, one might assume the speaker a person of no faith, particularly in view of the companion-poem printed on the page across from "Bethlehem Outcast": "Ballad of the Unmiraculous Miracle." The lines of the latter are almost as bleak as Hardy's about his temptation to go out into the wilderness on Christmas Eve in search of the crib, "Hoping it might be so." The mode is imperative:

> Sit under a pine on Christmas Eve,
> Heart bruised like a fallen nestling,

And the angels will sing you--no song save
The wind in the branches wrestling. . . .

Seek out a stable known of old
And see the oxen kneel--
With me crouched here before the cold
And hunger sharp as steel.

Go wander through the winter snows
And spy the Christmas bud
Unfold itself--the only rose
The brambles bear, my blood.

But the poem ends triumphantly, justifying its title:

Like wingless birds are wind and wood,
Well, oxen, flowering bush
Till Christmas Day when I see God
Plumaged in my plucked flesh.

(*WW*, p. 30)

As James Korges affirms of Miller in *Contemporary Poets*: "She does not wish to believe; she believes."(11) This faith is not an easy one: Korges continues: "Nor does she deny the hard realities and difficulties of writing about the religious experience, though she writes from the assurance of faith (perhaps even grace) and the stability of a fully civilized sensibility." (12) Her welding together of Bethlehem and Calvary here and elsewhere (e.g. "Christmas Mourning") helps Miller to transcend sentimentality.

The most impressive development of Christmas among all the religious lyrics appears in the five-part "Approaching Nada," published despite its brevity as a separate book in 1977. Set in Phoenix, Arizona, it displays brilliant symbolic landscape technique. The central section is given over to the liturgical celebration of

Christmas, in a manner about which Jane Cooper, reviewing *Onions and Roses*, remarks parenthetically: "(surely her more formal language and syntax derived from liturgy)." (13) The theme of silence returns movingly in lines inspired by the pre-Vatican II Introit for the Sunday within the Octave of Christmas, a beautiful excerpt from the Book of Wisdom: "When a profound stillness compassed everything/and the night in its swift course was half spent,/Your all-powerful Word, O Lord, bounded from heaven's royal throne."

This third section takes the form of a hymn to Christ as Phoenix:

> Many words do not compose the Word,
> nor do our dumbnesses make up the Silence
> whence Your Almighty Word leapt down
> "when night was in the midst of
>   / her still course. . .
> Allelulia!"
>
> Somewhere between silence and ceremony
>   / springs the Word,
> the wellhead of all hush feeding the roots
> of tongues, whether of men or angels,
>   / interchange
> between us and Your world. Listen, whoever
> tunes an ear.
>
> Sweet bird of Christmas singing all night long,
> Hamlet in part believed as I do wholly
> out of faith furnaced, fired by doubt,
> wings clipped by busy book and body,
>   / still, in You,
> my Phoenix!

(SNP, p. 123)

The fourth part, concerned with the mystics John

and Teresa, advances to Calvary, taking on the voice of Christ: "Follow me who flaunt/my body's banner/crimson before the bulls." The "nada" referred to in the title of the collection including the sonnet series is *The Cloud of Unknowing*, Van Ruysbroek's "dark silence" alluded to above, a condition chosen not only by the Spanish saints of "A Dream from the Dark Night" but by Miller herself:

> So poets, mystics of
> the bruising thing
> climb up bloody concretes
> to leave nailed high
> white pieces of themselves.
>
> (*SNP*, p. 125)

The name Miller selected for her anthology of stories and poems featuring the disabled, *Despite This Flesh*, hints at the gallantry with which she herself has entered into the mystery of suffering. How well she knows that out of it comes new life! Some of her strongest poems are on oneness with the crucified Lord: "No Return," "After Reading of Helen Keller," "The New Icarus," "Paradox," "Fantasia," "'Though He Slay Me,'" "Christopher," "Defense Rests," "Accepting," "Fantasy on the Resurrection," "The Resolution." Concluding *Wage War on Silence*, "Defense Rests," which consists of four haiku, pleads for a tangible love, no abstract thing but rather as concrete as "John's head on your breast or/Mary's lips on your feet. . ."; in the last haiku she defends her spiritual preference thus:

> If this
> is not enough--
> upon Your sweat, Your thirst,
> Your nails, and nakedness I rest
> my case.
>
> (*WW*, p. 69)

In this passage as always she uses capitals for pronouns relating to Christ, a formality extending to her choice of masculine over inclusive language in religious references. The particulars of the Crucifixion in "Defense Rests" illustrate her poetics as delineated in Nemerov's *Poets on Poetry*: "I have also fought a battle against abstraction, which, to my mind, is death to poetry." (15)

This force, silence, always more than the absence of noise, can be friend or foe: friend in the two poems, for instance, where Miller calls it mother ("Interim,""Study in White"), foe or at least somewhat hostile in "The Perpetual Penitent," "Temporary Relief," "Thorn in the Flesh," "A Mourning for Miss Rose," and "Waiting," with its mournful "The silence is only the sound/of my tongueless heart crying your name." In "The Worshiper" it combines diverse connotations, becoming a cloak for the lonely person praying. Janus-faced as silence is throughout the poetry, its omnipresence lends a tension which contributes to making Vassar Miller one of the most interesting literary figures of her century. Both for her victory over "the pain and ugliness of life" which art transforms into beauty and such silent music as Hopkins praises in "Elected Silence, sing to me. . .," she deserves homage.

Notes

Larry McMurtry: "Preface"
The Preface is an edited version of a speech that he gave at "A Tribute to Vassar Miller" at the University of Houston, October 10, 1983.

Frances Sage: "Vassar Miller: Modern Mystic"
1. *Texas Quarterly*, Summer 1978.
2. *Lucile*, Number 9, Fall 1977.
3. Line four is the revised version from *Selected and New Poems, 1950-1980*. The original line read "And You who can make eyes. . ."

Karla Hammond: "An Interview With Vassar Miller"
1. Schorer, Mark and Gordon McKenzie and Josephine Miles, eds. New York: Harcourt, Brace, 1945.

Paul Christensen: "Allowing For Such Talk"
1. *On A High Horse: Views Mostly of Latin American and Texas Poetry* (Fort Worth: Prickly Pear Press, 1983), p. 113.
2. *Ibid.*
3. A forty-minute version was delivered at the Fort Worth Museum of Art, but the essay itself was commissioned by *The Texas Observer*, which published it on October 23, 1981.
4. "Ever A Bridegroom: Reflections on the Failure of Texas Literature" (Austin: *The Texas Observer*, 1981), p.18-19.
5. *Ibid*, p.19
6. *Ibid*, p.19
7. *Ibid*, p. 10
8. McMurtry himself appears to have contradicted his own argument in writing his Pulitzer-award winning novel, *Lonesome Dove* (Simon and Schuster, 1985), which recounts the last days of a small ranch; originally written as a screenplay, it was rejected by its intended leads as portraying them unflatteringly in old age! It is not only McMurtry's most lyrical and moving account of rural life, but a variation on themes that run throughout Miller's poetry and the best of Southwestern literature.

9. "Ever A Bridegroom," p. 10.
10. *Ibid.*

Kenneth MacLean: "Crying Out: Aloneness and Faith in the Poetry of Vassar Miller"
1. Miller, Perry. *Errand into the Wilderness*, Cambridge: Harvard University Press, 1956. The title chapter is reprinted in *Theories of American Literature*, ed. Donald Kartiganer and Malcolm Griffith (New York: MacMillian Co., 1972), p. 11-23.
2. Reeve, Henry, ed. *Democracy in America*, New York: Alfred E. Knopf, 1945, Volume II, p. 76.
3. Harmon, Barbara Lee. *Costly Monuments*, Cambridge: Harvard University Press, 1982, intro., p. 18-22.
4. Nemerov, Howard, ed. *Poets on Poetry*, New York: Basic Books, 1966, p. 129.
5. *Ibid*, p. 121.
6. Norton, M.D. Herter, Trans. *Translations From the Poetry of Ranier Maria Rilke*, New York: W.W. Norton Co., 1962, p. 219.
7. Richardson, D.E. "Naked Acts by Southerners," *The Southern Review*, 21 (1985), p. 551.
8. Stitt, Peter. "The Art of Poetry IV," *The Paris Review*, 53 (1973), p. 201.
9. MacLean, Kenneth. "Berryman's 'Delusions'--On Poetry and Religious Pain," *A Book of Rereadings*, ed. Greg Kuzma, Lincoln, Nebraska: Best Cellar Press, 1980, p. 156-170.

Bruce Kellner: "Blood in the Bone: Vassar Miller's Prosody"
1. Kinsella, Thomas. *Another September*. Dublin, Ireland: Dolmen Press, 1958, p. 12.
Moore, Marianne. *Collected Poems*. New York: MacMillan, 1959, p. 12.
3. Auden, W.H. *The Dyer's Hand*. New York: Random House, 1962, p. 47.
4. *Ibid*, p. 22.
5. Hammond, Karla. "An Interview with Vassar Miller," *The Pawn Review*, VII: I (1983), p. 3.
6. *Ibid*, p. 4.
7. *Ibid*, p. 5.
8. "My Life As A Poet," unpublished manuscript, undated, author's collection.
9. Hammond, p. 9.

Thomas Whitbread: "Vassar Miller and Her Peers: A Causerie"
1. Stevens, Wallace. *Opus Posthumous*, New York: Alfred
A. Knopf, 1957, p. 16.
2. Williams, Oscar, ed. *The Pocket Book of Modern Verse*,
New York: Washington Square Press, 1960, p. 141.
3. Ellmann, Richard and Robert O'Clair, eds., p. 180-1.
6. *Ibid*, p. 175-6.
7. Foreword to *Selected and New Poems 1950-1980*, by
Vassar Miller, Austin: Latitudes Press, 1981), p. 7.
8. Eliot, T.S. *The Complete Poems and Plays*, New York:
Harcourt, Brace, 1952.
9. Stevens, Wallace. *Collected Poems*, New York: Alfred
A. Knopf, 1954, p. 507.
10. *Ibid*, p. 504-5.
11. Wilbur, Richard. *The Mind-Reader: New Poems*, New
York: Harcourt, Brace, Jovanovich, 1976, p. 28.

Robert Bonazzi: "Passionate Scriptures of the Body"
1. Kafka, Franz. *Dearest Father*. New York: Schocken
Books, 1968, p. 81.
2. Hammond, Karla. "An Interview with Vassar Miller,"
The Pawn Review, VII: I (1983), p. 14.
3. "A Poet's Eye View of Theology," unpublished manuscript, undated, author's collection.
4. Underhill, Evelyn. *Mysticism*. New York: E.P. Dutton
paperback edition, 1961, p. 11.

Sister Bernetta Quinn: "Vassar Miller's Anatomy of Silence"
1. Nemerov, Howard, ed. *Poets on Poetry*. New York and
London: Basic Books, 1966, p. 122.
2. Cooper, Jane. "Three Honest Poets and a Closet-
Laurentian." *The New York Times Book Review*, 22 December
1968, p. 10.
3. Nemerov, p. 129.
4. *Silent Music: The Science of Meditation*. New York:
Harper & Row, 1979, p. 67.
5. *Modern American Women Poets*. New York: Dodd,
Mead & Co., 1984, p. 348.
6. Nemerov, p. 117.
7. Ruysbrork, Jan Van. *The Spiritual Espousals*. Westmin-
ister, Md.: Christian Classics, 1983, p. 190.

8. Emory, Ann, ed. *Contemporary Authors*. Detroit: Gale Research Co., 1981, p. 22.

9. Maloney, George A. *The Silence of Surrendering Love*. New York: Alba House, 1986, p. 22.

10. Nemerov, p. 115.

11. Michael, Chester P. and Marie C. Norrisey. *Prayer and Temperament*. Charlottesville, Va.: The Open Door, Inc.,1984, p. 46.

12. Korges, James. *Contemporary Poets*. New York: St. Martin's Press, 1975, p. 36.

13. Cooper, p. 22.

14. Miller. Austin: University of Texas Press.

15. And it is never more so than in "Listening to Rain at Night," "where sound peels away from silence,/a cleavage no mind can perceive."

Steven Ford Brown: "A Vassar Miller Bibliography"

Parts of this bibliography are based on "A Vassar Miller Checklist" compiled by Helen G. Evans and Barbara Parrott Langdon of the Humanities Division, University Libraries, University of Houston. This checklist deals primarily with publications up to the 1968 publication of *Onions And Roses*. Research on publications since 1968 was assisted by access to the Vassar Miller Collection in the Special Collections at the University of Houston's M.D. Anderson Library.

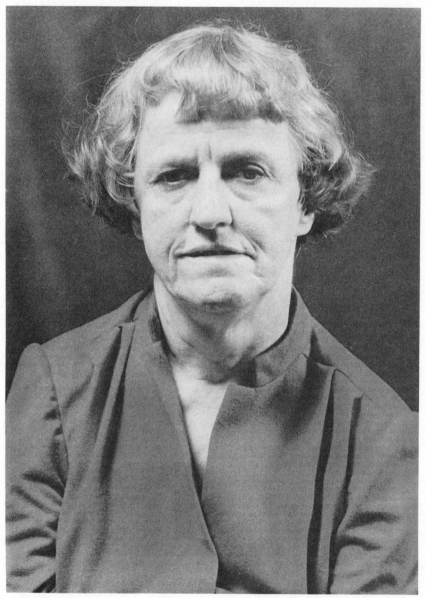

© 1982 by Nicholas Russell

Vassar Miller

Vassar Miller was born in 1924, in Houston, Texas, where she has lived all her life. She began writing as a child, fascinated by rhymes and wordplay. She earned B.S. and M.A. degrees from the University of Houston, completing her thesis on mysticism in the poetry of Edwin Arlington Robinson in 1950.

Miller taught creative writing at St. John's School and was writer-in-residence at the University of St. Thomas in 1975-76. In 1968 she participated in the Breadloaf Writers' Conference in Vermont and led the poetry workshop at the Southwest Writers' Conference in 1973 and 1983. Additionally, she has been involved in poetry workshops in Houston.

In 1961 Miller was nominated for the Pulitzer Prize for her book of poems, *Wage War on Silence* (Wesleyan University Press, 1961) and three of her books have won the annual poetry prize of the Texas Institute of Letters. In 1982 Miller was selected as alternate Poet Laureate for the state of Texas. She has published eight books of poetry and her poetry has appeared in more than fifty anthologies and hundreds of periodicals. *Library Journal* selected her volume, *Selected and New Poems 1950-1980* (Latitudes Press, 1981), as the best small press book of poetry for 1982.

Her poems have been translated into Spanish and published in Latin American journals. She has also written reviews and fiction. She is the editor of *Despite This Flesh* (University of Texas Press, 1986), an anthology of poetry and fiction by and about those handicapped with motor and sensory dysfunctions. Miller's most recent book of poems, *Struggling to Swim on Concrete*, was published in 1985 by the New Orleans Poetry Journal Press.

Bibliography

STEVEN FORD BROWN

nd = date of publication unknown
np = page numbers unknown

Primary Works

I. POETRY

A. Books

Adam's Footprint. New Orleans: The New Orleans Poetry Journal Press, 1956.
Wage War On Silence. Middletown: Wesleyan University Press, 1960.
My Bones Being Wiser. Middletown: Wesleyan University Press, 1963.
Onions And Roses: Middletown: Wesleyan University Press, 1968.
If I Could Sleep Deeply Enough. New York: Liveright, 1974.
Selected And New Poems, 1950-1980. Austin: Latitudes, 1981.
Struggling To Swim On Concrete. New Orleans: The New Orleans Poetry Journal Press, 1983.

B. Chapbooks

Approaching Nada. Houston: Wings Press, 1976.
Small Change. Houston: Wings Press, 1977.

C. Broadsides

"Irrevocable." Penny Poems from Midwestern University, Volume 3, Number 9, 14 March 1965.
"On Opening One Eye." Penny Poems from Midwestern University, Volume 4, Number 2, 30 April 1965.

"Open Question," Palaemon Broadside, Number 28 (1982).

"Private Weather Report." Penny Poems from Midwestern University, Volume 1, Number 3, 30 October 1964.

"Renewal." Penny Poems from Midwestern University, Volume 8, Number 2, 15 May 1967.

"The Better Part of Valor." Penny Poems from Amarillo College, Volume 1, Number 1, 20 June 1963.

"To Jesus on Easter." Penny Poems from Midwestern University, Volume 6, Number 2, 15 April 1966.

D. Anthologies

Benjamin, Edwin B., ed. *The Province of Poetry*, New York: The American Book Co., 1966.

Bens, John H. and Douglas R. Baugh, eds. *Icarus: Anthology of Literature*, New York: Macmillan, 1970.

Bogan, Louise, ed. *The Golden Journey*, New York: Reilly & Co., 1965.

Carruth, Hayden, ed. *The Bird/Poem Book*, New York: McCall Publishing, 1970.

Cooper, Jane, et. al., eds. *Extended Outlooks: The Iowa Review Collection of Contemporary Women Writers*, New York: Macmillan, 1981.

Corrington, John William and Miller Williams, eds. *Southern Writing in the Sixties: Poetry*, Baton Rouge: Louisiana State University Press, 1967.

Edwards, Margaret, ed. *Not Quite Twenty: Poems, Stories, And A Play*, New York: Holt, 1971.

Elknis, William R., Jack L. Kendall and John R. Willingham, eds. *Literary Reflections*, New York: McGraw-Hill, 1971.

Engle, Paul, and Joseph Langland, eds. *Poet's Choice*, New York: Dial Press, 1962.

Chase, Terry John and Sara Hannum, eds. *To Play Man Number One: Poems of Modern Man*, New York: Atheneum, 1969.

Cronin, James E., Maurice B. McNamee and Joseph A. Rogers, eds. *Literary Types and Themes*, New York: Holt, 1971.

Dallman, Elaine, et. al., eds. *Woman Poet: The South*, Las Vegas: Women in Literature, 1987.

Garrett, George, ed. *The Girl in the Black Raincoat*, New York: Duell, Sloan and Pearce, 1966.

Graham, Don, ed. *South by Southwest: Stories From Modern Texas*, Austin: University of Texas Press, 1986.

Hall, Donald, Robert Pack and Louis Simpson, eds. *New Poets of England and America*, New York: Meridian Books, 1957.

Hazo, Samuel, ed. *A Selection of Contemporary Religious Poetry*, Glen Rock, N.Y.: Paulist Press, 1963.

Lask, Thomas, ed. *The New York Times Book of Verse*, New York: Macmillan, 1970.

Lynch, Peggy, ed. *Hide and Horn*, Austin: Eakin Press, 1986.

Nemerov, Howard, ed. *Poets on Poetry*, New York: Basic Books, 1966.

Owen, Guy and William Taylor, eds. *Southern Poetry Today*, Deland, Fla.: Owen and Taylor (Impetus Chapbook No. 2), 1962.

Pouncey, Lorene, ed. *The Houston Poetry Fest Anthology*, Houston: The Houston Center for Humanities, 1985.

Ramsey, Paul, ed. *Contemporary Religious Poetry*, Mahwauh, N.J.: Paulist Press, 1986.

Richardson, H. Edward and Frederick B. Shroyer, eds. *Muse Fire: Approaches to Poetry*, New York: Knopf, 1971.

Stokesbury, Leon, ed. *The Made Thing: An Anthology of Contemporary Southern Poetry*, Fayetteville: The University of Arkansas Press, 1987.

Saylors, Rita, ed. *Liquid City*, San Antonio: Corona Publishing Co., 1987.

Tufte, Virginia, ed. *High Wedlock Then Be Honoured*, New York: Viking, 1970.

Turner, Alberta, ed. *50 Contemporary Poets*, New York: David McKay Co., 1977.

Untermeyer, Louis, ed. *Modern American Poetry*, New York: Harcourt, Brace and World, 1962.

Walsh, Chad, ed. *Today's Poets: American and British Poetry Since the 1930's*, New York: Scribners, 1964.

Williams, Oscar, ed. *A Little Treasure of Modern Poetry, English and American*, New York: Scribners, 1970.

II. FICTION

Uncollected Stories

"Autumn Come Silent." *Latitudes*, Spring 1972, p. 54-59.
"Good Lunar Watch." *Whetstone* (Huntsville, Texas), Fall 1969, p. 35-38.
"Pack." *Shenandoah*, Winter 1963, p. 41-47; reprinted in *South By Southwest*, ed. Don Graham. Austin: University of Texas Press, 1986.
"Tea Party." *Midwestern University Quarterly*, 1966, p. 45-53.

III. ANTHOLOGIES

Books

Despite This Flesh (as editor). Austin: University of Texas Press, 1984.

IV. CRITICISM, INTERVIEWS, REVIEWS

Birth Rites (Foreword), by Mario Zuniga, Bryan, Texas: Cedarshouse Press, 1984.
"From Thunder to Sputters." Review of *Diamond Cut Diamond*, by Ewart Milne; *The Sorrows of Cold Stone*, by John Malcolm Brinnin; *The New Barbarian*, by Withrop Palmer; *Illegitimate Sonnets*, by Merrill Moore; and *Musical Chairs*, by James Broughton. *Hopkins Review*, Fall 1951, p. 79-86.
Hammond, Karla. "An Interview with Vassar Miller," *The Pawn Review*, 1983, p. 1-18.
Hammond, Karla. "An Interview with Vassar Miller," *The Pikestaff Forum*, Spring 1984, p. 7-8.
"Houston Poet Cynthia MacDonald Innovative Teacher as Well as Poet." *The Houston Post*, 4 February 1973, Spotlight Section, p. 8.
"A Resonance of Grace." Review of *The Resonance of Grace*, by James Newcomer, *Vortex*, Spring 1986, p. 27.

Review of *A Letter From Li Po and Other Poems*, by Conrad Aiken. *The New Orleans Poetry Journal*, July 1956, p. 28-30.

Review of *Dance Without Shoes*, by William Pillin. *The New Orleans Poetry Journal*, May 1957, p. 36-38.

Review of *Delta Return*, by Charles Bell; *The Second Man and Other Poems*, by Louis O. Coxe; *The Scattered Causes*, by Samuel Morse; *The Rudiment of An Eye*, by W. Price Turner; *The Kitchen Dance*, by Robert Hutchinson, and *Two Sides of A Poem*, by Katherine Bellamann. *The New Orleans Poetry Journal*, October 1956, p. 23-30.

Review of *Poets Today III*; and *Nice Diety*, by Martha Baird. *The New Orleans Poetry Journal*, January 1957, p. 37-45.

Review of *The Timid Phoenix*, by Chris Bjerknes; *The Gentle Weight Lifter*, by David Ignatow; and *Birthdays From the Ocean*, by Isabella Gardner. *The New Orleans Poetry Journal*, October 1955, p. 28-31.

Review of *Unexpected Truce*, by Don Geiger; and *The Town Not Yet Awake*, by Dorothy Cowles Pinkney. *The New Orleans Poetry Journal*, September 1957, p. 38-42.

"Various Visions." Review of *A Change of World* , by Adrienne Cecile Rich; *A Garland About Me*, by George John; *Private Speech*, by Philip Freund; *How Smoke Gets Into the Air*, by Terrence Heywood; and *The Scientist and Other Poems*, by Hans Juergensen-Steinhart. *Hopkins Review*, Spring-Summer 1953, p. 197-200.

"What Is A Poet?" *Poets On Poetry*, ed. Howard Nemerov. New York: Basic Books, 1966, p. 114-132.

Whitebird, Joanie and Christopher Woods. "An Interview With Vassar Miller." *Touchstone*, Spring 1986, p. 4-15.

V. VIDEOTAPE

"A Tribute to Vassar Miller." (Music, Readings, Various Speakers) Welcome W. Wilson, Elizabeth Wachendorfer, Dr. Charles E. Bishop, Eleanor Tinsley, Rosellen Brown, Stanley Plumly, William Matthews, Beverly Lowry, Larry McMurtry, Ed Morris, Mary Starnes and Margaret Tucker. Recorded October 10, 1983 at the University of Houston; Houston: Friends of the University of Houston Libraries, 1983.

Secondary Sources

I. ARTICLES

Anon. "Cover Story." *Whetstone*, Fall 1969, p. 2.

Anon. Editorial on University of Houston Tribute to Poet Vassar Miller. *The Houston Post*, 6 October 1983, sec. B, p. 2.

Anon. "Local Writers Win Honors." *Houston Chronicle*, 2 February 1957, sec. A, p. 7.

Anon. "May Get Title." *The Houston Chronicle*, 1 February 1961, sec. 3, p. 8.

Anon. Photograph and biographical comment accompanying publication of "Mystery." *The Houston Post*, 28 January 1962, sec. 8, p. 3.

Anon. "Poet Wins Headliner Award." *The Houston Post*, 6 May 1969, sec. 2, p. 4.

Anon. "The Remarkable Miss Pennybacker" (Discussion of Miller in article on her creative writing teacher.) *Extra: The University of Houston Alumni Magazine*, March 1961, p. 6-7.

Anon. "University of Houston to Present Tribute to Houston Poetess Vassar Miller." *The Houston Post*, 11 September 1983, sec. F, p. 12.

Anon. "Vassar Miller Receives Top Honor at Press Breakfast." *The Houston Chronicle*, 5 May 1969, sec. 4, p. 2.

Anon. "Vassar Miller's Poems Win in Annual Contest." *The Houston Chronicle*, 30 October 1949, sec. A, p. 2.

Baird, Joseph. "Breathing New Winds: Poems With Arresting Images and A New Perception of the Disabled." *Disabled USA*, 1984, p. 2.

Bedell, W.D. "Texas Letters Prizes." *The Houston Post*, 26 February 1961, sec. 1, p. 1.

Bennett, Elizabeth. "UH Homage to Poet Vassar Miller Featured." *The Houston Post*, 16 October 1983, sec. G, p. 3.

Bennett, Elizabeth. "She Fought Rough Odds to Forge A Special Life." *The Houston Post* (*Parade* Supplement), 22 August 1982, p. 20-21.

Daughtery, Tracey. "The Spirit Soars." *The Texas Observer*, 11 November 1983, p. 20-21.

Doehring, Gaye. "Praise and Paradox." *Extra: The University of Houston Alumni Magazine*, February 1966, p. 8-12.

Dressman, Fran. "Profile of A Poet." *Pride: The Magazine of the University of Houston*, October 1983, p. 10-11.

Feldman, Claudia. "Miller Overcomes Dry Spells to Earn Recognition as Local and International Author of Quality Verse," *The Houston Chronicle*, 9 October 1983, sec. 6,p.3.

Harrigan, Stephen. "Write 'Em Cowboy." *Texas Monthly*, December 1976, p. 158-165.

Hastings, Sue. "Houston Poet Believes Religion Gives Meaning." *The Houston Chronicle*, *Zest* Supplement, p. 8 (nd).

Kass, Miriam. "Accept Me Though I Give Myself Like A Castoff Garment..." *The Houston Post*, 26 Jan. 1969, p.1-4.

Lipscomb, Maude. *Innerview*, April 1985, sec. 1, p. 14.

McCorquodale, Ellen. "Nominee for Pulitzer Prize Has No Schedule for Writing." *The Houston Post*, 8 January 1961, sec. 7, p. 2.

McMurtry, Larry. "Ever A Bridegroom: Reflections on the Failure of Texas Literature." *The Texas Observer*, 23 October 1981, p. 1-19.

Milligan, Bryce. "At Long Last Texas Poets Come of Age." *The Dallas Morning News*, 26 October 1984, p. 1AA-2AA.

Mulvany, Tom. "Physical Courage and Great Ability Led Vassar Miller to the Pinnacle." *The Houston Chronicle*, 8 December 1969, sec. 2, p. 1.

Owen, Guy. "Vassar Miller: A Southern Metaphysical." *Southern Literary Journal*, Fall 1970, p. 83-87.

Sage, Frances. "Contemporary Women Poets of Texas." *The Texas Quarterly*, Summer 1978, p. 84-108.

Sage, Frances. "Vassar Miller: Modern Mystic." *Latitude 30° 18'*, 1982, p. 95-109.

Standafer, Shirley. "A Poet Has To Have A Certain Sensitivity." *The Houston Chronicle*, 29 July 1970, sec. SE, p. 4.

Stewart, Susan. "Vassar Miller: The Lone Literary Star." *The Dallas Times Herald*, 6 December 1981, p. 7.

Tucker, Chris. "The Seeker." *Houston City Magazine*, February 1982, p. 41-81.

Tucker, Chris. "Vassar Miller, Conquering Life's Injustice with Poetry." *The Dallas Morning News*, 20 December 1981, p. 4G.

Untermeyer, Louis. "The Poet as Patron." *Wilson Library Bulletin*, 36 (1962), p. 370.

Wade, Sidney. "Her Own Dilemma: Vassar Miller." *The Texas Humanist*, January/February 1984, p. 34-36.

Waldron, Ann. "Houston's Own Prize Winning Poet, Vassar Miller." *The Houston Chronicle*, 2 February 1975, *Zest*, p. 12.

Wood, Susan. "Vassar Miller To Be Honored at Reading at CAM." *The Houston Chronicle*, 20 June 1976, *Zest*, p. 8.

II. REVIEWS

A. *Adam's Footprint*

Eckman, Frederick. *Poetry*, 90 (1957), p. 386-97.

Nemerov, Howard. *Kenyon Review*, 20 (1958), p. 25-37.

Williams, George. *The Houston Chronicle* (nd, np).

Wright, James. *Sewanee Review*, 66 (1958), p. 657-668.

B. *Wage War On Silence*

Book Review Digest, January 1962 (np).

Ehrenpreis, Irwin. *The Minnesota Review*, 1 (1961), p. 362-72.

Fitts, Dudley. *The New York Times Book Review*, 26 (February 1961), p. 10-12.

Fowler, Helen. *Approach*, 44 (Summer 1962), p. 40-42.

Friedman, Norman. *Chicago Review*, 19 (June 1967), p. 64-90.

Garrett, George. *The Houston Post*, 26 February 1961, p. 34.

Hay, Sarah Henderson. *Vocies*, 175.(May-August 1961), p.39-42.

King, Ethel. *Catholic Library World*, May-June 1961, p. 519.

Pendleton, Conrad. *Prairie Schooner*, 35 (1961), p. 363-64.

Spector, Robert D. *Saturday Review*, 11 February 1961, p. 67.

Tobin, James Edward. *Spirit: A Magazine of Poetry*, 29 March 1962, p. 26-31.

Weil, James L. *Sparrow*, 18 (November 1962), p. 22-23.

Wright, James. *Poetry*, 99 (1961), p. 178-83.

C. *My Bones Being Wiser*

Book Review Digest, August 1964 (np).

Burke, Herbert. *Library Journal*, 89 (1 January 1964), p. 116.
Carruth, Hayden. *Hudson Review*, 2 May 1964, p. 34-36.
Fowler, Albert. *Approach*, 51. (Spring 1964), p. 33-42.
Friedman, Norman. *Chicago Review*, 19 (June 1967), p. 64-90.
Gelpi, Albert J. *The Southern Review*, 3 (1967), p. 1024-35.
Levertov, Denise. *The New York Times Book Review*, 21 June 1964, p. 1;-12.
Stafford, William. *Poetry*, 104 (1964), p. 104-108.
Tindall, Theodore. *Voices*, 184 (May-August 1964), p. 50-51.
The Times Literary Supplement, 18 June 1964, p. 532.

D. *Onions And Roses*

Book Review Digest, January 1969 (np).
Choice, 5 (1968), p. 1310.
Cooper, Jane. *The New York Times Book Review*, 22 December 1968, p. 10-11.
Dillard, R.H.W. *The New Orleans Review*, 1 (1968-69), p. 15.
Guest, William F. *The Houston Post*, 2 March 1969, p. 15.
Lieberman, Laurence. *Poetry*, 114 (1969), p. 40-58.
Miller, Marcia. *Library Journal*, 93(15 September 1968) p. 3145.
Ricks, C. *The Massachusetts Review*, Spring 1970, p. 313.
Stillwell, R. *Michigan Quarterly Review*, Fall 1969, p. 278.
Virginia Quarterly Review, 45 (Winter 1969), p. XIX.
The Times Literary Supplement, 17 October 1968, p. 1172.

E. *If I Could Sleep Deeply Enough*

Best Sellers, 34 (15 February 1975), p.506
Booklist, 71 (15 June 1975), p. 1046
Brunsdale, Mitzi M. *The Houston Post*, 16 February 1975, *Spotlight*, p. 32.
The Burlington Free Press, 20 December 1974, p. 36
Choice, 12 (May 1975), p. 393.
The Christian Century, 92 (30 April 1975), p. 447.
The Dallas Morning News, 12 January 1975, p. 7C.
Etter, Dave. *American Libraries*, November 1974,. p. 548.
Grumbach, Doris. *The New Republic*, 4 January 1975, p. 32.
Kiser, Thelma Scott. *The Ashland Daily Independent* (nd, np).
The Hartford Times, 5 January 1975 (np)

Langdon, James. *The New Orleans Times Picayune*, 2 March 1975, sec. 3, p. 9.
Osing, Gordon. *The Commercial Appeal*, 19 January 1975, sec 6, p. 6.
Quartet, Fall 1976, p. 38-39.
Williams, Deborah. *Library Journal*, 15 December 1974, p.3203.
Wood, Susan, *The Houston Chronicle*, 15 December 1974, p.8.

F. *Approaching Nada*

DeGregori, Thomas. *The Houston Chronicle*, 5 March 1978, p. 16.

G. *Small Change*

Anderson, Michael. *The Pawn Review*, Spring 1977, p. 66-67.
Choice, 13 (February 1977), p. 1597
Library Journal, 101 (15 December 1976), p. 2543
McAnally, Mary. *New Letters*, Fall 1979, p. 115-116.

H. *Selected and New Poems, 1950-1980*

Christensen, Paul. *The Texas Observer*, 6 August 1982, p. 16-17.
Colquitt, Betsy. *The Fort Worth Star Telegram*, 1986 (np)
Hall, Joan Joffee. *The Houston Post*, 16 May 1982, sec. AA, p.23.
Library Journal, 107 (15 December 1982), p. 2305.
Robertson, Foster. *The Librarians Browser*, Fall 1982, p. 15.

I. *Struggling To Swim On Concrete*

Library Journal, 109 (15 November 1984), p. 2115.
Lopate, Philip. *The Houston Post*, 22 July 1984, sec. FA, p. 10.
Richardson, D.E. *The Southern Review*, 21 (1985), p. 547-553.

J. *Despite This Flesh*

Beck, Father Albert. *The Texas Catholic Herald*, 14 September 1984, p. 27.

Bryant, Richard L. *Journal of the American Medical Association*, 2 May 1986, p. 2363.

Kliatt Young Adult Paperback Book Guide, 20 (Winter 1968), p. 33.

Library Journal, 110 (1 September 1985), p. 199.

The Los Angeles Times, 29 September 1985, p. 3.

McDermott, Marise. *The Texas Journal*, Fall/Winter 1985/86, p. 48-49.

III. BIOGRAPHICAL AND REFERENCE

A Directory of American Poets, New York: Poets and Writers, Inc., 1975, 1987.

Etheridge, James M. and Barbara Kopala, eds. *Contemporary Authors*, Detroit: Gale Research Co., 1965, Vol. 11-12, p. 269.

Pouncey, Lorene. *American Women Writers*, Vol. 3, New York: Frederick Ungar Publishing Co., 1981, p. 187-188.

Untermeyer, Louis. *Modern American Poetry*, New York: Harcourt, Brace and World, 1962, p. 678-79.

Vinson, James, ed. *Contemporary Poets*, New York: St. Martin's Press, 1975, p. 1053-54.

Walsh, Chad. *Today's Poets: American and British Poetry Since the 1930s*, New York: Scribners, 1964, p. 422.

Wakeman, John, ed. *World Authors 1950-1970*, New York: The H.W. Wilson Co., p. 997-998.

The Writer's Directory 1976-1978, London: St. James Press; New York: St. Martin's Press, 1976.

Women's Poetry Index, Phoenix: Oryx Press, 1985.

Notes on Contributors

Robert Bonazzi has edited Latitudes Press since 1966. He is the author of *Living the Borrowed Life* (New Rivers Press, 1974), *Fictive Music* (Wings Press, 1979), and *Perpetual Texts* (Latitudes Press, 1986). A new book of poetry *There Must Be A Way* is scheduled for publication in 1987 by Latitudes Press. He is presently editing several books on the life and work of John Howard Griffin for JHG Editions/Latitudes Press.

Paul Christensen is the author of the important critical study, *Charles Olson: Call Him Ishmael* (University of Texas Press, 1979) and of five collections of poetry. His essays and articles on modern poetry have appeared in such journals as *The American Book Review*, *Parnassus*, *The Southern Review*, *The Texas Observer*, and *The Texas Quarterly*. A professor of modern American literature at Texas A & M University, he is presently writing a critical study of the poetry of Clayton Eshleman and a history of Texas poetry.

Frances K. Sage grew up in Montana, studied poetry at the University of Montana under Richard Hugo, and completed her doctorate in English at the University of Texas. She has been co-editor of *Latitude 30° 18'* and has published an essay, "Contemporary Women Poets of Texas," in *The Texas Quarterly*. She presently lives in Austin, Texas.

Karla Hammond was for a number of years the staff interviewer for *The Bennington Review*. Her interviews also appeared in such journals as *The American Poetry Review*, *Confrontation*, *Helix* (Australia), *Northwest Review*, *Parnassus*, *The Southern Review* and *Western Humanities Review*. Her interviews with such writers as Margaret Atwood, Olga Broumas, June Jordon, Maxine Kumin, Marge Piercy, May Sarton and Leslie Ullman have been collected into a book, *Away From Silence: Interviews with Contemporary Women Poets*.

Bruce Kellner is professor of English at Millersville University in Lancaster, Pennsylvania. He has also been a guest lecturer at the University of Vienna and was an educational consultant at Warnborough College at Oxford in 1986. His books include *Carl Van Vechten and the Irreverent Decades* (University of Oklahoma Press, 1968), *The Harlem Renaissance: An Historical Dictionary for the Era* (Greenwood Press, 1984; reprinted by Methuen Press, 1987), and *Letters of Carl Van Vechten* (as editor, Yale University Press, 1987). He is presently completing a reference book on Gertrude Stein to be published by Greenwood Press in 1988.

Kenneth MacLean is an Associate Professor of English at Seattle University. He is a frequent reviewer and author of articles on modern and contemporary American poetry. He is also the author of a chapbook of poetry, *The Long Way Home* (1982), and has a longer volume, *Blue Heron's Sky*, in preparation.

Larry McMurtry was born in Wichita Falls, Texas, and grew up on a ranch near there. He received his M.A. from North Texas State University and his M.A. from Rice University; he also studied at Stanford University. He is the author of numerous books, which include a book of essays, *In A Narrow Grave*, the novels, *Horse-*

man Pass By, which is also known as *Hud*, after the title of the motion picture adaptation, *Leaving Cheyenne*, *The Last Picture Show*, *Terms of Endearment*, and *Texasville*. His novel, *Lonesome Dove*, won the 1986 Pulitzer Prize for fiction.

Sister Bernetta Quinn, O.S.F., whose critical evaluations of Randall Jarrell and Ezra Pound were among the first such appraisals, is currently completing two very different books, the fruit of several years of scholarship: *Pilgrimage to the Stars: A Young Person's Dante* and *Randall Jarrell in Retrospect*. Her previous books include *The Metamorphic Tradition in Contemporary American Poetry* (Rutgers University Press, 1955), *Randall Jarrell: A Critical Study* (Twayne Publishers, 1978), and *Ezra Pound: A Critical Study* (Columbia University Press, 1985).

Thomas Whitbread teaches English and American literature at the University of Texas. His books of poetry include *Four Infinitives* (Harper & Row, 1964) and *Whomp and Moonshiver* (Boa Editions, 1982).

STEVEN FORD BROWN

Steven Ford Brown was born in 1952 in Florence, Alabama, and grew up in Birmingham. He received his B.A. in English from the University of Alabama in Birmingham, where he edited several literary journals, assisted in the university reading series, and taught contemporary poetry for the Special Studies Division from 1981 to 1983. He has also taught in the Poets-In-The-Schools Program, been the co-producer of an award-winning program on poetry for public radio, and coordinated research for "The Writer In Society" series on PBS. With Pedro Gutierrez Revuelta, he has translated two books by the Spanish poet Angel Gonzalez, *American Landscapes and Other Poems* and *Against Time*.